# Making Music in the Primary School

*Making Music in the Primary School* is an essential guide for all student and practising primary school teachers, instrumental teachers and community musicians involved in music with children. It explores teaching and learning music with the whole class and provides a framework for successful musical experiences with large groups of children.

Striking the perfect balance between theory and practice, this invaluable text includes case studies and exemplars, carefully designed activities to try out in the classroom, as well as a range of tried-and-tested teaching strategies to help you support and develop children's musical experience in the classroom.

Grounded within a practical, philosophical and theoretical framework, the book is structured around the four key principles that underpin effective music teaching and experience:

- Integration – how can we join up children's musical experiences?
- Creativity – how can we support children's musical exploration?
- Access and Inclusion – how can we provide a relevant experience for every child?
- Collaboration – how might we work together to achieve these aims?

Written in a clear, accessible and engaging style, *Making Music in the Primary School* will give you all the confidence you need when working with whole classes, whatever your musical or teaching background.

**Nick Beach** is Deputy Director of Performing and Creative Arts, Trinity College London, UK.

**Julie Evans** is 7–14 and 11–18 PGCE Music Course Leader, Canterbury Christ Church University, UK.

**Gary Spruce** is Senior Lecturer in Education with responsibility for Music ITT, The Open University, UK.

# Making Music in the Primary School

## Whole class instrumental and vocal teaching

## Edited by Nick Beach, Julie Evans and Gary Spruce

Routledge
Taylor & Francis Group

LONDON AND NEW YORK

This first edition published 2011
by Routledge
2 Park Square, Milton Park, Abingdon, Oxon OX14 4RN

Simultaneously published in the USA and Canada
by Routledge
711 Third Avenue, New York, NY 10017

*Routledge is an imprint of the Taylor & Francis Group, an informa business*

Typeset in Galliard by
GreenGate Publishing Services, Tonbridge, Kent
Printed and bound in Great Britain by
TJ International Ltd, Padstow, Cornwall

*British Library Cataloguing in Publication Data*
A catalogue record for this book is available from the British Library

*Library of Congress Cataloging-in-Publication Data*
Making music in the primary school : whole class instrumental and vocal
teaching / [edited and selected by] Nick Beach, Julie Evans, and Gary
Spruce. -- 1st ed.
p. cm.
1. School music--Instruction and study--Great Britain. 2. Education,
Primary. I. Beach, Nick. II. Evans, Julie, 1958- III. Spruce, Gary.
MT3.G7.M37 2011
372.87'044--dc22
2010026233

ISBN: 978-0-415-56129-7 (hbk)
ISBN: 978-0-415-56130-3 (pbk)
ISBN: 978-0-203-83457-2 (ebk)

# Contents

# Figures

# Tables

# Contributors

**Nick Beach** studied at Dartington College of Arts, the National Centre for Orchestral Studies and Middlesex Polytechnic. Nick has worked as a peripatetic violin teacher and has also held several Music Service management posts, most recently as Head of Education with Berkshire Young Musicians Trust. He currently holds the post of Deputy Director of Performing and Creative Arts for Trinity College London. Nick was closely involved in the development of the KS2 Music CPD Programme and the Arts Awards and leads Trinity's professional development work worldwide. As a practising musician Nick is a violinist and conductor.

**Philippa Bunting** is a teacher of wide experience, having worked in a wide range of environments from initial experiences of whole class instrumental teaching on the Tower Hamlets String Project to, currently, leading the First String Experience course at the Royal Academy of Music. She also has a strong background in teacher training, presently at the RNCM, and works as a freelance music education consultant.

**Rita Burt** is Programme Director for the Trinity Guildhall/The Open University KS2 Music CPD Programme. Prior to this she was Head of the Music Service and Music Advisor for the London Borough of Barking and Dagenham for eight years. During her time there she developed her passion for whole class instrumental and vocal work at KS2 through the national pilot wider opportunities programme in 2002–2004. Previously she taught music in secondary schools for 20 years.

**Madeleine Casson** is Course Leader for the KS2 Music CPD Programme provided by Trinity Guildhall and The Open University and the Training and Development Manager for Charanga, whose eLearning system is used by music services and music teachers across the UK. As well as teaching and performing regularly she undertakes a wide range of freelance projects.

**Carolyn Cooke** is Lecturer in Education at The Open University with specific responsibility as a subject leader on the University's flexible PGCE Music course. Previously she was Head of Music in a large comprehensive secondary school as well as being a Regional Subject Advisor in the South East for the recent National Curriculum changes.

**Julie Evans** has been a music teacher and head of department in five secondary schools. She has also had extensive experience as an instrumental teacher of both violin and piano. She is currently Senior Lecturer in Music at Canterbury Christ Church University where she is responsible for the 7–14 and 11–18 PGCE Music courses.

**Margaret Griffiths** trained at the Royal Academy of Music, Reading University and London University Institute of Education. She taught for 12 years in secondary schools and then became a teacher trainer at London University. At the same time she was heavily involved with examination boards at the time of the introduction of the GCSE. In 1985 she joined Her Majesty's Inspectorate of schools as a music specialist. She was Ofsted's specialist adviser for music from 2000. During her time as an HMI she was responsible for annual published reports on music in primary and secondary schools; teacher training; and music services, as well as a range of government initiatives in music education. In her spare time, Margaret studied for an MBA and a Diploma in French. She has also been for many years a singer, conductor, repetiteur and accompanist. Margaret retired in December 2006 and is now a freelance music education specialist, as well as Granny – or adopted Aunt – to many music education practitioners in England. She works closely with the Federation of Music Services and is a national evaluator for a number of government-funded music education programmes.

**Chris Harrison** is a music education consultant whose work includes teaching on ITE courses at London Metropolitan and Greenwich Universities, running courses for teachers and young musicians, and writing educational materials. He is a past Chair of NAME, and is currently managing editor (publications) for the association. His musical tastes are wide-ranging and he performs with a number of groups and ensembles. He is particularly interested in the role of improvisation in learning music and in developing musical activities in the community at large.

**Francesca Matthews** works for Trinity College London as Area Leader for the Trinity Guildhall/ The Open University KS2 CPD Programme. She studied as a singer at Trinity College of Music, worked for a London music service before going into secondary teaching, and then became workshop leader and Education Advisor for English Pocket Opera and Glyndebourne Opera House. Francesca is a workshop leader for organisations such as the Royal Opera House and Sing Up, and delivers INSET for Local Authority music services. She is also a tutor on The Open University PGCE course. She continues to sing professionally both on the jazz circuit and as a studio session singer.

**Lis McCullough** is a freelance music education consultant and researcher living in Northumberland. Originally a primary school class teacher, she worked for many years as a primary music advisory teacher and was Chair of the National Association of Music Educators 2008–2009. Her MA dissertation investigated children's development in composition while her doctoral research explored class teachers' beliefs and attitudes concerning music in education.

**Tim Palmer** is Senior Lecturer in Music Education at Trinity College of Music, where he specialises in Creative Project Leadership. He has led education projects for many of the UK's leading arts organisations, and has just finished a two-year post as Musician in Residence at the National Maritime Museum. Tim regularly performs as a percussionist with many of the UK's orchestras.

**Chris Philpott** taught music and performing arts in English secondary schools for 16 years before moving into higher education. His writing is focused on the pedagogy of teacher education in music. He is currently Head of the School of Education and Training at the University of Greenwich and in his spare time he plays cricket.

**Gary Spruce** is Senior Lecturer in Education at The Open University. His primary responsibility is as subject leader for the university's PGCE Music course. Presently, he is also involved in a programme of professional development for those teachers involved in whole class instrumental and vocal teaching developed in partnership with Trinity College London. He has written widely on music education and presented papers at national and international conferences. He is a practising musician with a particular interest in music for the theatre.

**Vanessa Young** is Principal Lecturer in Education at Canterbury Christ Church University where she coordinates primary music within the Education Faculty. She has had a wide range of involvement in music education in relation to both CPD and ITE. She also has extensive experience in staff development. Her writing and research in relation to music includes teaching styles in music and teacher development. She is co-editor of *Primary Music Today* – a magazine for primary school teachers of music.

**Katherine Zeserson** is responsible for the strategic design, direction and implementation of the Sage Gateshead's internationally acclaimed Learning and Participation programme. She has a national reputation as a trainer and music educator in a wide range of community, educational and social contexts including pre-school settings, primary and secondary classrooms, voluntary sector organisations, and higher and further education postgraduate and professional training programmes. She has held many arts-in-education residencies, working with both primary and secondary age children. She performs regularly as a singer with the a cappella ensembles Mouthful and Woman Music.

**Sally Zimmermann** is Music Adviser at the Royal National Institute of Blind People. Previously, she was a class music teacher in secondary and special schools in London and a peripatetic violin teacher and a private piano teacher. She is a guest lecturer in Special Needs at the Institute of Education, London University. Her *Instrumental Music* was published in 1998. Recent music making includes a classical/rap fusion project, leading a large male voice group and improvisations with adults with learning disabilities.

# Foreword

*Margaret Griffiths*

> Music is feelings, isn't it, miss?

This recent quotation is from a nine-year-old boy as he left an exciting whole class string session and went almost 'bouncing' to his next lesson. His reactions seem to represent the heartland and purpose of whole class instrumental programmes for all young people in primary schools. In these lessons, instrumental learning gives all young people opportunities to experience the sense of achievement and enjoyment that comes from making individual progress in the context of making music together. The nationally funded Wider Opportunities programmes for pupils in primary schools have enabled us to move, from a largely individual – or isolated – approach to music instrument learning, to an integrated and corporate one. This means that individual technical and music skills are nurtured within the context of developing all aspects of what it is to be musical.

The range of genres and traditions from which music making experiences are now drawn is huge. We have moved away from the term 'classical music' and instead use 'music for classical instruments' since the repertoire of our large mixed ensembles can now cover up to 400 years of music! The music we offer to children reflects the vibrant and diverse nature of music today, valuing the 'classics' alongside music from the widest range of cultures and traditions.

We now expect all our young people to have access to making music in the same way as they have access to learning to read, to write and to count. Without this access, we cannot reliably offer the choices which need to follow and which enable our young musicians to set out on their own preferred musical pathways. We must also ensure that all young people – whatever their needs – have equal access to the new and open opportunities which music provision can offer, and in which they can thrive.

Music is a specific phenomenon – a simultaneously complex, ephemeral and abstract world of sounds – hence the 'feelings' and responses it inspires and creates. Its teaching requires highly skilled and committed practitioners in whose care our children's music making can flourish; and who themselves should also expect to continue learning.

There is still much work to be done to bring agreement over what we mean by high qualities in pedagogy; in ensuring that there is a smoother transition into the secondary phase from KS2; and using partnerships and resources to achieve the best provision possible. The creative exploration and development of music technologies remains an exciting challenge; as does our ability to support all staff with high quality professional development programmes.

The contributors to this book are nationally distinguished practitioners, whose commitment is to an integrated music education of the highest quality for all. The specialist writing should act as a catalyst for consolidation for the majority of our colleagues – and for a change of heart, as well as a change of practice, for the rest. Our young people – and the adults who work with them – deserve no less.

# Introduction

As we enter the second decade of the twenty-first century, a quiet revolution is taking place in the way children experience instrumental and vocal music making in many primary schools in England. Gone are the days when instrumental tuition has been available only to the select few. Now, children learn instruments in whole classes in order to make music together, not just as performers, but as composers, improvisers and critical listeners, and are supported in their musical learning by class and instrumental teachers working together. In the UK such teaching is commonly referred to as whole class instrumental and vocal teaching (WCIVT) or Wider Opportunities.

This new approach to musical learning presents significant challenges for all teachers. The 'master and apprentice' model of instrumental teaching, which has been widely accepted for centuries as the most appropriate and effective one for developing performing skills, cannot simply be transferred to the large group and whole class context. Instrumental teachers and community musicians who have extensive experience of teaching individuals or small groups will find they need to develop a new range of teaching strategies and approaches when working with whole classes. Similarly, classroom teachers and support staff who are experienced in teaching in whole classes may mistakenly feel that their lack of formal musical training means they cannot support children's musical learning.

The purpose of this book is to support all teachers in developing their skills, knowledge and understanding within a practical, philosophical and theoretical framework, underpinned by proven and accepted principles of good practice.

These principles are:

- *Integration* – an approach to music education which acknowledges and makes links between all those aspects of what it is to be musical and all those places in which children learn about and experience music;
- *Creativity* – placing creative teaching and learning at the heart of music education;
- *Access and inclusion* – providing a rich and relevant musical learning experience for all children which acknowledges their backgrounds, aspirations and interests;
- *Collaboration* – class teachers, instrumental teachers and musicians in the community working together with a shared vision of what music education should be.

The principles are not 'stand alone' but are integrated and reflect aspects of each other. So, for example, the principle of 'collaboration' establishes that class instrumental teaching is at its best where instrumental teachers, classroom practitioners and musicians work collaboratively so that children experience a joined-up approach to music learning. This is then reflected through the 'integration' principle which is founded upon the ideals of a holistic approach to music education which values a range of contributions to a child's musical development from formal and non-formal contexts. Both of these might be said then to feed into the 'access and inclusion' principle. This principle recognises the importance of addressing each child's needs, aspirations and entitlements. This is achieved through valuing their music making and their ways of engaging with music, and acknowledging the musical learning and understanding they bring with them from outside of school as well as the richness of music making and musical practices in the world beyond the classroom.

These principles provide a framework for the development of a pedagogy for WCIVT which can meet the challenges of:

- breaking down divisions that have traditionally existed in music education between various 'providers' both within and beyond formal education structures;
- providing children with authentic musical experiences which draw on the pedagogical models, musical processes and practices from a wide range of musical cultures and traditions;
- conceptualising instrumental/vocal tuition as a means through which children develop their understanding of all aspects of what it is to be musical, focusing on the learning child rather than the instrument.

Meeting these challenges has implications for those working in, and being educated for, work in music teaching. It challenges a number of preconceptions about the roles, relationships and responsibilities of teachers, certain conventional views about the nature and purpose of music education (and particularly instrumental teaching and learning) and the value we place on different approaches to teaching and learning.

The book is structured under the four principles outlined above framed by two chapters which place WCIVT in its historical and contemporary context and a concluding chapter which looks at the role of assessment in supporting learning and teaching. Each of the main sections has a 'Setting the scene' chapter which sets out the broad issues and introduces the chapters within the part. This structure allows each of the four principles to be investigated from a range of viewpoints. The book is not meant to be read as a primer or a theoretical exposition but rather as a book which teachers and musicians can actively engage with. To this end, the book includes case studies, exemplars and activities which invite the reader to try out or explore the ideas that are contained within the chapters in their own professional context. These are carefully designed so that whatever the reader's musical or teaching background they will be of relevance in supporting children's musical learning.

The book has its roots in a programme of continuing professional development (CPD) for teachers, developed by The Open University and Trinity College London with funding from the UK government's Department for Children, Schools and Families. The purpose of the programme is to support teachers and other music practitioners working on Wider Opportunities programmes through online learning, workshops and peer mentoring.

# Part 1

# Setting the context

# Chapter 1

# How did we get here?

## The historical and social context of whole class instrumental and vocal teaching

*Julie Evans*

## Introduction

This chapter aims to consider the history of how children have learnt to sing and play instruments in large groups and whole classes, both within and beyond the curriculum. It is important to establish that much instrumental and vocal learning has always taken place (and continues to do so) in informal contexts with skills being passed on from one generation to the next, mainly through an aural tradition. In the West, from medieval times onwards, formal instrumental and vocal teaching and learning was important in both church and court contexts and from the eighteenth century onwards such formal learning was additionally available via private tuition and in conservatoires. The predominant model for this instrumental and vocal teaching was the 'master and apprentice' model with an emphasis on one-to-one tuition and the imparting of skills from an expert to a novice, and this model continues to be influential even today. What might be less evident is that, in the context of the English education system, children have learnt to sing and play instruments in large groups and whole classes for a surprisingly long time and quite systematically since the nineteenth century.

## The establishment of music in schools

Music has not always been valued in English schools. Before about 1840 the study of music in schools was almost non-existent, but Russell states that from the 1840s onward

> there were always a number of teachers entering the profession who were at least partially qualified in the teaching of music. But the scope, quality, and indeed the actual existence of school music was still almost entirely dependent upon the whim of individual teachers, and there were undoubtedly many schools in which music had no place in the curriculum.
>
> (Russell 1987: 44)

Despite the fact that there is now a national curriculum for music in England some of these statements may still apply.

An important development in the early 1840s was the introduction of the sol-fa system into English schools by proponents such as John Hullah, John Curwen and Sarah Glover. In England in the early nineteenth century a surprisingly large proportion of the population were involved in choral singing and became able to sight-sing through reading tonic sol-fa. Hullah, Curwen and Glover each developed a slightly different system, Hullah using a 'fixed doh' principle and Curwen and Glover a moveable doh where the tonic of any new key was always 'doh'.

Each system was based on the principle that 'traditional' stave notation was hard to read and that tonic sol-fa allowed musical reading issues to be overcome. Those currently teaching whole classes to sing or play still have to grapple with similar concerns about what notations are accessible or even necessary for children to progress in their musical learning.

The Education Act of 1870 established a national system of state education but music was often excluded in schools as a curriculum subject because it did not receive a subsidy. Eventually music was included and it was even decided that any state elementary school *not* including music on its syllabus would lose funding. Initially, a heavy emphasis was placed on singing and the acquisition of musical aural and literacy skills. Plummeridge suggests: 'With the establishment of a national educational system, choral activity and music reading were encouraged in schools, partly in the hope that such action would eventually lead to an improved standard of musical performance in church services' (Plummeridge in Philpott 2001: 5). Russell also states that 'its great appeal to both educationalists and many music specialists lay in its cheapness, and above all its value as a vehicle for moral education' (Russell 1987: 45).

Parallels can again be drawn with recent thinking. The *Music Manifesto Report No. 2* (DfES 2006) emphasises that singing is for everyone and, whilst it does not discuss moral education, it does state that singing can build communities and contribute to better mental and physical health. Some of the results were more tangible, and Russell (1987) suggests that, by 1891, 60 per cent of children in English and Welsh elementary schools were being taught to sing from one form of notation or another.

It is a common misconception that most of the singing that took place in late nineteenth-century schools was of hymns and sacred music. In fact the Education Code sought to ensure that state schools were non-denominational. The singing of folk songs was common but some suggested that these songs displayed 'frank vulgarity' and

> when the debate over music in education moved increasingly from a moral to an artistic basis, there was further criticism that the songs, normally learnt by ear and sung in unison, were damaging the quality of sight-reading and part-singing.
>
> (Russell 1987: 46)

The educationalist Arthur Somervell encouraged the production of the *National Song Book* (1906) which used many British 'national songs' from the seventeenth and eighteenth centuries, as opposed to folk songs. As Cox suggests:

> The strength of the book lay in its substantial selection from all four nations of the kingdom, as well in the sheer scope of a project including 200 songs. It represented the triumph of the orthodoxy of the national song, as opposed to the more recently discovered folk song. The collection became universally used in schools.
>
> (Cox 1993: 78)

Thus singing was established as a central music curriculum activity and this remained the case throughout the next century.

## Instrumental teaching and learning in schools

From the end of the nineteenth century many schools and authorities moved beyond teaching just vocal music and the violin became the main school instrument that was taught. In 1898 a system was initiated by Murdoch and Company at All Saints National School in Maidstone which became known as the 'Maidstone System'. The company provided a violin on hire purchase for three pence per week and arranged for tuition at a further three pence a week. In 1907 William McNaught (in Russell 1987) saw an estimate claiming that 10 per cent of English children were receiving school violin tuition and by 1909 Murdoch and Company claimed to have supplied violins to 400,000 pupils in over 500 schools. The 'Maidstone System' undoubtedly contributed to the formation of school orchestras at the beginning of the twentieth century and many of these orchestras were comprised almost solely of violins. A National Union of School Orchestras was established and claimed to have involved 100,000 pupils by 1906.

The violin proved a popular school instrument because it was inexpensive and portable but similar schemes based on piano tuition were not successful. The cost of instrumental lessons was a problem even at the beginning of the twentieth century. McNaught carried out an investigation of instrumental tuition in Bradford schools in 1898 and found that, although in some schools almost half of pupils were learning to play an instrument, in schools attended by poorer children 'the percentage learning instruments is, as may be expected, very low – sometimes in the boys schools as low as one per cent. The obstacle to instrumental instruction is entirely one of pounds, shillings and pence, and most especially pounds' (Russell 1987: 47).

Despite the success of these innovative large group teaching projects they were largely decimated by the effects of the First World War. However, the recorder emerged as another instrument that could easily be learnt by whole classes. Arnold Dolmetsch was a pioneer of the use of early instruments, including the harpsichord and recorder. He realised the potential that the recorder could have in music education as it was easy for a beginner to produce a good tone. Having initially made wooden recorders with his own design of mouthpiece, Dolmetsch, in collaboration with Boosey and Hawkes, went on to mass produce instruments in plastic rather than wood and schools were then able to afford to bulk buy them. This enabled generations of school children to learn to play the recorder.

## Music appreciation, extra-curricular music and grade examinations

Alongside singing and recorder playing, music appreciation became an important whole class activity in the period after the First World War and this was clearly related to the development of the wireless and gramophone. This emphasis on an essentially passive musical activity was certainly detrimental to practical musical engagement by whole classes. Another development was the area of 'extra-curricular' musical activities and this was particularly true in independent and grammar schools where choirs, orchestras and bands began to flourish. This was a major development which had some not entirely positive consequences since, as Gordon Cox suggests: 'We can see a foreshadowing of the gulf that was later to become characteristic between the "extra-curricular" and classroom work' (Cox 1993: 135).

Performance examinations were also firmly established by this time, having been offered by Trinity College of Music since 1876 and soon after by the Associated Board of the Royal Schools of Music (ABRSM). Pitts believes: 'As well as setting the precedent that serious musical skills could only be acquired from a private, expensive teacher, such a system advanced the notion that music was not for everybody, but only for the skilled or wealthy' (Pitts 2000: 11).

## Beyond performance

Until this time making music in schools centred on performance. In the 1940s a major development in instrumental teaching and learning in schools was the pioneering of the Percussion Band movement, led by Louie de Rusette. In percussion bands, children played parts on drums, tambourines and triangles, whilst a pianist supplied the melodic and harmonic texture. A key feature was that the children acted as conductors. More importantly, Rusette believed that the children should be encouraged to express themselves through rhythm, melody and harmony and not just imitate music, stating: 'We shall not become a musical nation until music is treated as a creative art in the Primary school' (Rusette in Philpott and Plummeridge 2001: 13). This was a forward-looking view of the potential of instruments in the classroom.

Cox believes that 'in schools, instrumental music was clearly in the ascendant' (Cox 2002: 15) at this time and he suggests that music teachers had a whole range of classroom instruments available to them including percussion band instruments, stringed instruments, recorders and bamboo pipes. Margaret James had set up the Pipers' Guild in 1932, based on work carried out in a school in Fulham using pipes similar to those she had seen in Sicily. The philosophy of the society was that arts such as handicraft, design and music making are natural and universal and her pupils made, decorated and played their instruments. James stated that 'when the music, craft and art teachers are determined to combine their efforts to bring about a home-made orchestra, there will be creative music in schools' (James in Cox 1998: 242).

Another guild intended to develop children's instrumental learning was the Bow-Craft Guild which was established in 1937. By 1948 its aims were

> to provide a complete and co-ordinated Scheme for the Development of Instrumental Music in Schools by means of Violin Classes, leading to the School Orchestra: embracing also the early stages of Rhythmic and Melodic Training through Percussion Band and Recorder Classes.
>
> (Cox 1998: 242)

Also in 1948 Reginald Hunt maintained that 'instruments provided a great deal of value in the teaching of musical literacy' and suggested the piano class as perhaps the most practical method, arguing that 'the keyboard was a more tangible and precise aid in this respect than the voice' (Hunt in Cox 2002: 16).

An association called the Music Education of the Under-Twelves (MEUT) Association grew out of the philosophy of the Percussion Band movement. It was established in 1949 and played a part in the development of primary school music education until its demise in 1983. The association felt that many teachers tended to concentrate on one element of the musical menu, for example the percussion band, pipe playing or eurhythmics. Gordon Cox states: 'It was one of the purposes of the Association to help provide a balanced musical diet, so that children could move, sing, play music and read it, and come to know the literature of music' (Cox 1998: 240).

This was further advocacy of the creative potential of instrumental learning. The possibility of children engaging in kinaesthetic activity as part of 'a balanced musical diet' sprang from the work of Emile Jacques-Dalcroze who visited England in 1912 when eurhythmics became a common whole class activity at this time. There are examples of schools linking movement with melodic creativity on instruments and this reflected Dalcroze's philosophy:

> The real innovation in the Dalcroze method … was to use movement to approach notions that up until then had only been taught intellectually or technically. With this method, musical concepts are experienced and internalized by what Jacques-Dalcroze called the sixth sense, the kinesthetic sense.
>
> (Comeau 1995: 40)

*Music and Movement* broadcasts were pioneered by the BBC and were used extensively in schools.

In the 1950s many children were able to learn instruments through the Orff method. Orff was a German composer and educator who was determined that the students of dance and gymnastics that he worked with should create their own music for dance and movement. At first the only instruments available to them were various forms of drums and untuned percussion. Orff began pitched work with the piano, recorders and lower-pitched instruments but wanted to widen his palette of sound and to find instruments that were technically less demanding. He had the instruments of the gamelan in mind, but it was the chance gift of an African marimba that led to the design and manufacture of a simplified form of xylophones, to which metallo-phones and glockenspiels were added. These instruments are still commonly found in English classrooms and all over the world. Orff's method encouraged children to compose, which was very different from the previous recreative performance model.

Local authority music services were established in England and Wales from the 1950s onwards. Music services were responsible for the provision of instruments and instrumental teachers, as well as high quality vocal tuition, in schools in their authority. The provision still perpetuated the 'master and apprentice' model and group teaching was unusual, with groups tending to be small and usually no larger than four pupils. Additionally, almost every music service developed a youth orchestra which was seen as the pinnacle of instrumental achievement.

In the 1970s instrumental and vocal teaching, within and beyond the curriculum, offered pupils a plethora of opportunities. Within the curriculum, teachers could choose to use a wide variety of instruments and the electronic keyboard began to become a staple instrument. The traditional percussion band declined but the classroom orchestra was common, with teachers using commercially produced and 'home-grown' resources. Teachers who did make their own arrangements for their classroom orchestras were able to include pupils with limited skills as well as experienced musicians. However, there was no national curriculum for music in England at this time and pupils' entitlement from school to school was hugely varied.

An innovative whole class string project was initiated in the 1970s by Sheila Nelson in Tower Hamlets. Nelson suggests: 'String players good enough to supply a healthy youth orchestra programme in London were in short supply' (Nelson 1985: 69). She had studied the work of Paul Rolland in the USA, an inspirational teacher who had taught string playing to large groups of children in a school system. Nelson's first beginner group of about 20 children was chosen on a 'hands up who would like to play' basis from the entire junior section of two primary schools, which resulted in a mixture of seven- to ten-year-old learners. They received one lesson per week and were allowed to take home the instruments. The group learned together, with assistance from several teachers who helped the children to develop correct physical movement patterns. Cellos joined the violins for the part of the lesson which involved shared repertoire, but went off to another room for the rest of the time with a cello teacher. After several experi-mental years Nelson decided that optimum learning was gained by starting groups of seven- to eight-year-olds. It was realised that it was important to fully integrate music reading by using sol-fa reinforced by whole body actions, rhythm cards and French time names and Nelson wrote specific musical materials for the Tower Hamlets project. A regular second lesson was introduced each week in a smaller group which allowed reinforcement of the content of the big group lesson. This meant that the pupils were more likely to retain information, although Nelson describes the lessons as 'very brief'. She makes the important point: 'The instrumental lessons had by now become part of the normal school curriculum, although still provided by visiting teachers. It became increasingly necessary to build up a well-integrated relationship with the fulltime staff of any school we worked in' (Nelson 1985: 74).

It was eventually decided that two years was a useful initial learning period, after which children were encouraged to continue. The number of children continuing varied but Nelson noted a correlation between the enthusiasm of the headteacher and the number of children continuing. She also states: 'Class teachers who attend the string lessons, sometimes even to learn alongside the children, are an invaluable support' (Nelson 1985: 74). This observation was important and continues to hold true, even if curriculum teachers see themselves as non-specialist music teachers.

At its height the Tower Hamlets project involved over 1,000 young string players, 20 schools in and around the Tower Hamlets area and 35 qualified string teachers. The project resulted in admirable *musical* learning taking place. As Keith Swanwick remarks:

> The complexities of playing a stringed instrument were not tackled by narrowing down attention to one way of approaching music or by confining activities to one style of practising or to hacking through a tutor book page by page. Musical learning in these schools took place through multi-faceted engagement: singing, playing, moving, listening to others, performing in different size groups, integrating the various activities we associate with music. Those teachers responsible for bringing this about saw their job as teaching music through an instrument, not just teaching the instrument.
>
> (Swanwick 1994: 144)

Other large group instrumental learning initiatives used 'band programmes' which were imported from America. In such programmes large groups of pupils were taught to play wind and brass instruments using specially devised materials that meant that different instruments could learn to play the same pitches simultaneously and promote playing in ensembles at a very early stage of learning. Such programmes were often driven by economic considerations, but benefits to the learners, such as increased motivation gained through learning with peers, became evident.

## Popular and world musics

Within the curriculum in the 1980s popular music started to be widely used and this had a clear and positive effect on instrumental and vocal learning. As Salaman suggests: 'So obviously are the children involved in their work, questions as to whether pop music is the child's natural milieu or an abomination matched only by bubble gum and space invaders seem irrelevant' (Salaman 1983: 49). Additionally, music from around the world became a common feature of curriculum music making but it is interesting that the majority of instrumental teaching beyond the curriculum is still focused on Western classical instruments.

By the beginning of the 1990s vocal and instrumental teaching was well established in British schools. Many and varied approaches had been tried but not necessarily sustained. In curriculum music lessons children learnt to sing and play instruments such as recorders, percussion instruments, some popular and world music instruments and the ubiquitous electronic keyboard. It was also estimated that approximately half a million children were receiving vocal and instrumental tuition (Sharp in Philpott 2001: 224). Vocal and instrumental tuition continued to be provided through local authority music services, private organisations and self-employed music teachers and this was often in the form of individual or small group lessons.

## References

Comeau, G. (1995) *Comparing Dalcroze, Orff and Kodaly: Choosing Your Approach to Teaching Music*. Ontario: Centre franco-ontarien de ressources pédagogiques.

Cox, G. (1993) *A History of Music Education in England 1872–1928*. Aldershot: Scolar Press.

Cox, G. (1998) 'Musical Education of the Under-Twelves (MEUT) 1949–1983: Some aspects of the history of post-war primary music education', *British Journal of Music Education*, 15(3): 239–253.

Cox, G. (2002) *Living Music in Schools 1923–1999: Studies in the History of Music Education in England*. Aldershot: Ashgate Publishing Limited.

Department for Education and Skills (DfES) (2006) *Music Manifesto Report No. 2: Making Every Child's Music Matter*. London: The Stationery Office.

Nelson, S. (1985) 'The Tower Hamlets Project', *British Journal of Music Education*, 2(1): 69–93.

Philpott, C. (2007) *Learning to Teach Music in the Secondary School*. London: Routledge.

Philpott, C. and Plummeridge, C. (eds) (2001) *Issues in Music Teaching*. London: RoutledgeFalmer.

Pitts, S. (2000) *A Century of Change in Music Education: Historical Perspectives on Contemporary Practice in British Secondary School Music*. Aldershot: Ashgate Publishing Limited.

Russell, D. (1987) *Popular Music in England, 1840–1914*. Manchester: Manchester University Press.

Salaman, W. (1983) *Living School Music*. Cambridge: Cambridge University Press.

Swanwick, K. (1994) *Musical Knowledge: Intuition, Analysis and Music Education*. London: Routledge.

# Chapter 2

# The contemporary context of whole class instrumental and vocal teaching

*Julie Evans*

## Introduction

The contemporary context of whole class instrumental and vocal teaching (WCIVT) is exciting and developing very rapidly. A 'blizzard of initiatives' (a politician's words) is allowing pupils in mainstream primary schools in England to have access to more extensive opportunities to sing and to play a musical instrument than previous generations. Pupils are working in collaboration with musicians from beyond their school, including instrumental teachers and visiting artists. Challenges have arisen from these developments. New approaches to teaching and learning are being adopted as pupils learn to play or sing as a whole class, links are being established with pupils' musical learning in the curriculum and beyond the school, and secondary schools are beginning to build on the experiences that pupils bring with them from their primary schools.

This chapter aims to establish the contemporary context of whole class instrumental and vocal teaching, particularly focusing on:

- the developments that have occurred over the last two decades in establishing commonalities between whole class instrumental and vocal teaching (WCIVT) and the National Curriculum for Music for England and Wales;
- specific government funding for whole class instrumental and vocal teaching.

## The national curriculum and 'a common approach'

A statutory National Curriculum (NC) for Music in England and Wales was established in 1992 and, as a foundation subject, music became a compulsory curriculum subject for pupils up until the end of Key Stage 3. From the outset it was intended that music making within and beyond the curriculum should be intrinsically linked, and in the *Music for Ages 5 to 14 (Final Report)* on the National Curriculum it is stated:

> Instrumental teachers should be fully aware of the point that their pupils have reached in the general music curriculum, of the detailed scheme of work involved, and of the tasks and materials used in the classroom. The instrumental music lessons should be regarded as an alternative form of delivery, not as an adjunct or optional extra.
>
> (DES 1991: 58)

The Music Advisers' National Association (MANA) produced a forward-looking document, *Instrumental Teaching and Learning in Context: Sharing a Curriculum for Music Education* (MANA 1995). The document reinforced the point that instrumental tuition had been regarded as a 'bolt-on' to the music curriculum, undertaken by a few, taught in isolation from mainstream music and delivered in a style which often bore no relation to the teaching and learning taking place in the broader music education programme adopted within the class or, for that matter, in other curriculum areas.

(MANA 1995: 3)

It was proposed that the areas of aural awareness, technique, interpretation, composing, communication and critical awareness from the 1995 NC Orders for Music were entirely compatible with those for a balanced instrumental curriculum. MANA believed that, to ensure coherence in pupils' learning across the whole breadth of their musical experiences, instrumental and class teachers needed to consider ways in which instrumental learning could complement and enhance curriculum music. It was equally emphasised that there was a need for class music to enrich and reinforce instrumental learning (MANA 1995: 6).

Building on this philosophy, the Federation of Music Services (FMS) and the National Association of Music Educators (NAME) produced a document called *A Common Approach: A Framework for an Instrumental/Vocal Curriculum* (FMS/NAME 1998). It emphasised the ideal that all children should have the opportunity to sing and to play a musical instrument. The framework attempted to provide a common approach to planning a coherent and progressive curriculum for instrumental/vocal teaching, one that complemented and reflected the requirements of the National Curriculum. Playing and singing lay at the heart of the framework and, as with the National Curriculum, performing and composing, listening and appraising were encompassed at each stage. The premise of sound before symbol was also emphasised. Subsequently, in 2002 FMS, NAME and the Royal College of Music (RCM) produced a series of documents which were complementary to *A Common Approach* and which were instrument family-specific called *A Common Approach 2002: An Instrumental/Vocal Curriculum*. *A Common Approach* resulted in a more consistent approach across music services to planning for pupils' progression in instrumental and vocal learning and it facilitated links between pupils' music making in curriculum music and in music lessons beyond the classroom.

## The 'wider opportunities pledge'

Despite these developments, because of changes in funding to music services, there was an abrupt decline in the provision of instrumental tuition by the mid-1990s. This prompted a strong response and the issue was widely discussed in the press by eminent musicians such as Pierre Boulez and Simon Rattle. Plummeridge and Adams state:

> Musicians and educationalists have reacted sharply to what is regarded as a worrying state of affairs; many express the fear that one of the most valued and successful post-war developments in school music education is in danger of being irrevocably damaged by short-sighted financial policies ... Music educationalists argue that limiting students' access to instrumental tuition is a regressive step and contrary to the principle of equal opportunities; the point is also made that lack of provision will ultimately have a negative effect on the musical life of the nation.

(Plummeridge and Adams in Philpott 2001: 224)

In 1997 the government responded to these concerns about the decline of instrumental teaching and reaffirmed its commitment to music in schools. Two major developments were the establishment of the Standards Fund for Music, which was intended to ensure that all children would be able to pursue and develop their interests and talents, and the Youth Music Trust (now Youth Music), which aimed to improve and expand music outside of the curriculum. The Standards Fund for Music particularly ensured that substantial sums were allocated for the improvement and expansion of music services.

In the 2001 White Paper *Schools Achieving Success* the government pledged to ensure that, 'Over time, all primary pupils who want to will be able to learn a musical instrument' (DfES 2001: 12) and this became known as the 'Wider Opportunities Pledge'. The commitments of the pledge are actually quite vague. 'Over time' suggests no specific time frame, it is not entirely clear how pupils will volunteer to learn an instrument and, very importantly, *any* musical instrument can be learnt. Despite this vagueness, the pledge has had a huge impact and there have been some innovative responses to the pledge.

In 2002 Youth Music, in collaboration with the DfES (Department for Education and Skills), set up 13 pilot programmes to demonstrate how the provision of specialist instrumental tuition could be expanded to involve higher numbers of pupils in KS2. The QCA produced complementary units of work to show how instrumental tuition could extend and enrich the National Curriculum for Music. The main aims of the programmes were:

- to give as many pupils as possible access to specialist instrumental tuition during KS2 for a trial period;
- to provide new musical experiences for large numbers of pupils before they embark on specialist tuition;
- to provide pupils with musical skills and experiences which form secure foundations and which prepare them for individual choices.

The majority of these 'Wider Opportunities' programmes targeted whole classes or large groups of pupils. The Ofsted evaluation document *Tuning In: Wider Opportunities in Specialist Instrumental Tuition for Pupils in Key Stage 2* (Ofsted 2004) suggested that having a confident and expert 'music leader' working with a team of teachers and tutors proved to be the most successful way to establish, consolidate and develop the pilot programmes and that some of the best work occurred where the music leader was both a curriculum specialist and an experienced instrumental tutor. In many programmes successful new partnerships were formed between the school-based music staff, music service tutors and professional musicians and some of the best results were obtained where all three worked together to co-teach large numbers of pupils. The projects in the Wider Opportunities pilot encouraged group music making in a wide variety of genres, including African drumming, traditional Indian music and steel pans. All these projects were inclusive, engaged large numbers of performers and allowed consideration of the pupils' enculturation.

By 2004 ten per cent of the KS2 school population had been involved in Wider Opportunities programmes. By 2008 Hallam *et al.* (2007) suggested that over half of all KS2 pupils were involved in a Wider Opportunities programme. In 2002 two-thirds of pupils learning with music services were being taught Western classical instruments but the 2004 survey stated that pupils were being offered learning opportunities on a variety of instruments across a wide range of styles and genres, including world musics, folk and popular music. Wider Opportunities programmes have certainly encompassed a wide range of musical styles and genres and programmes have included the learning of more unusual instruments such as ukuleles, ocarinas and even junk percussion instruments made by pupils themselves. This broadening of what instrumental and vocal teaching and learning can include is a very positive result and means that children have access to and can be involved in learning to sing and play instruments in styles, genres and traditions that have real relevance to them.

Recognising that this entitlement to instrumental learning meant the development of new approaches, the government, via the DfES, gave substantial funding in 2007 to a continuing professional development programme for those involved in the delivery of music at KS2, particularly whole class instrumental and vocal programmes. This successful and innovative programme offered face-to-face workshop sessions, online resources and support and personal mentoring for each participant (www.ks2music.org.uk). By 2010 over 4,000 teachers had participated in the programme.

In 2008 the Schools Minister confirmed £322 million of government funding for music during the period 2008–2011 and reiterated that the government's most important priority was the extension of free musical tuition to all primary school pupils, for at least a year, to be achieved nationwide by 2011. The government's *Guidance on the Music Standards Fund Grant 1.11 2008–11* states: 'By 2011 we believe that all primary school pupils who want to *can* have the opportunity to learn a musical instrument' (DCSF 2008: 1). The Schools Minister also unveiled a radical new orchestral programme called In Harmony. This was inspired by the hugely successful Venezuelan project El Sistema which began in 1975 when Jose Antonio Abreu began giving music lessons to children from shanty towns in Caracas, Venezuela. Abreu believes that learners from deprived communities are given opportunities, through music, to move out of poverty. He believes: 'Music will sow in the child and the young a spirit of accomplishment, excellence, a cult for the beautiful, the fair, the just, the noble; and will transform the personality' (Abreu quoted in *The Washington Post*, 15 December 2006).

El Sistema became so successful that the Venezuelan government realised its potential and the Ministry of Health and Social Development supported the project. There are now hundreds of orchestras for children and young people throughout Venezuela and more than a quarter of a million children are involved.

In a press notice the DCFS stated that in the In Harmony projects:

> Children from the most deprived parts of the country will be taught musical instruments by charismatic, high quality music teachers. They will then be brought into full scale orchestras and encouraged to play live in front of audiences from an early age. Children as young as four might play concerts as part of these orchestras.
>
> (DCSF 2008)

The government allocated funding of £3 million over three years to pilot In Harmony projects in Liverpool, Norwich and Lambeth in South London.

The traditional model of instrumental teaching on a one-to-one basis and with children expected to practise in their own homes for substantial periods until they are at a standard where they might join an ensemble is not one that always suits children from deprived backgrounds. The Venezuelan approach is one of immersion, and children get together several times a week and have musicians with them constantly when they play. Sistema Scotland's first pilot project (a project similar to In Harmony in England) began in June 2008 in Stirling. It has embedded these principles and has already had a huge impact not only on the pupils involved but the whole local community. Whether In Harmony programmes will proliferate and have equal success in the way that they did in South America remains to be proven. It will be interesting to observe whether the social impact can be as immense on British children whose deprivation is, perhaps, somewhat different from that of children in South America.

Singing and vocal tuition have not been neglected. In the *Music Manifesto Report No. 2: Making Every Child's Music Matter* (DfES 2006) Howard Goodall makes the powerful statement:

> Singing is as natural and enjoyable to human beings as laughing. It is easy and universal, bonding us first to our mothers and then to each other. It complements our grasp of language and communication and accelerates our learning processes. It does not belong exclusively to one culture or another and cannot be traced, like musical instruments, through some distant family tree back to one place, time or tribe. It is the cheapest form of musical expression and where most children's musical journey begins.
>
> (DfES 2006: 30)

In the *Music Manifesto Report No. 2* the government's intention to develop a 'singing nation' was established. Subsequently an initiative called Sing Up was launched which was a national programme of singing activity for primary school children which aimed to ensure that good quality singing was central to young children's lives in primary schools, in the home and in the wider community. Sing Up stated that its aim was that 'We want singing to be at the heart of every school' (www.singup.org) and it suggested: 'Every child deserves the chance to sing every day. Singing improves learning, confidence, health and social development. It has the power to change lives and help to build stronger communities'.

The programme offered a wide range of training through courses and workshops. Online resources included an extensive 'Song Bank' which contained a wide variety of songs, all with audio tracks and accompanying activities, together with suggestions for how to teach the songs effectively.

Pupils across England have had the opportunity to be involved in some way with Sing Up. This may have been through singing songs from the Sing Up song bank, by being involved in performances which have resulted in their school gaining a Sing Up award or simply through taking part in more regular singing as teachers gain confidence in leading singing as a result of taking part in the range of CPD opportunities that Sing Up has offered.

Recent funding and developments have firmly established whole class vocal and instrumental teaching in England. This has meant that musicians and music educators have had to re-evaluate the musical and other benefits of learning to sing or play in a whole class or large group. The long-established conservatoire model of musical tuition being all about developing a virtuoso solo performer who develops technical proficiency through regular practice has been challenged. Whole class and large group teaching undoubtedly offers other benefits to learners, even if these are not always as immense as the social benefits demonstrated in the El Sistema projects. Hallam (1998: 253) believes that group tuition can:

- be more stimulating for teachers and pupils;
- provide more opportunities for demonstrating alternative methods and strategies;
- provide more opportunities for critical evaluation, both musical and technical;
- foster independent learning in pupils;
- be more fun;
- provide opportunities for informal performance to assist with overcoming nervousness;
- help shy children to feel less inhibited playing with others.

Swanwick sums up the potential of whole class and group teaching:

Music making in groups has infinite possibilities for broadening the range of experience, including critical assessment of the playing of others and a sense of performance. Music is not only performed in a social context but is learned and understood in such a context. Music and music learning involves building up plans, images, *schemata*, through ways of thinking, practising, playing and responding; learning by imitation of and comparison with other people. We are strongly motivated by observing others and we strive to emulate our peers, often with a more direct effect than being instructed by those persons designated as 'teachers'.

(Swanwick 1994: 151)

It would appear that the contemporary context of whole class instrumental and vocal teaching is a positive one, and as Gordon Cox states:

What is hopeful about much of the present situation is that with recent developments including the Standards Fund, Youth Music, the Music Manifesto, and the Musical Futures initiative, the previously separate worlds of classroom music, extra-curricular music, instrumental teaching and music in the community appear to be establishing connective pathways.

(Rainbow with Cox 2006: 385)

We are certainly at a point where most children of primary age in England will have had *more* opportunities than previous generations to learn to sing or play an instrument. We need to continue to work to ensure that their learning experiences are of the highest quality possible, increasing the 'connective pathways' and developing effective pedagogy.

## References

Department for Children, Schools and Families (DCSF) (2008) *Guidance on the Music Standards Fund Grant 1.11 2008–2011.* London: The Stationery Office.

Department for Education and Skills (DfES) (2001) *Schools Achieving Success.* London: DfES.

Department for Education and Skills (DfES) (2006) *Music Manifesto Report No. 2: Making Every Child's Music Matter.* London: The Stationery Office.

Department of Education and Science (DES) (1991) *Music for Ages 5 to 14 (Final Report).* London: DES.

Federation of Music Services and National Association of Music Educators (FMS/NAME) (1998) *A Common Approach: A Framework for an Instrumental/Vocal Curriculum.* London: Faber Music.

Federation of Music Services, National Association of Music Educators and the Royal College of Music (FMS/NAME/RCM) (2002) *A Common Approach 2002: An Instrumental/Vocal Curriculum.* London: Faber Music.

Hallam, S. (1998) *Instrumental Teaching: A Practical Guide to Better Teaching and Learning.* London: Heinemann.

Hallam, S., Creech, A., Rogers, L. and Papageorgi, I. (2007) *Local Authority Music Services Provision 2007 for Key Stages 1 and 2. Research Report DCSF-RR014.* London: DCSF.

Music Advisers' National Association (MANA) (1995) *Instrumental Teaching and Learning in Context: Sharing a Curriculum for Music Education.* London: MANA.

Office for Standards in Education (Ofsted) (2004) *Tuning In: Wider Opportunities in Specialist Instrumental Tuition for Pupils in Key Stage 2.* London: The Stationery Office.

Philpott, C. (2001) *Learning to Teach Music in the Secondary School.* London: RoutledgeFalmer.

Rainbow, B. with Cox, G. (2006) *Music in Educational Thought and Practice* (new edn). Woodbridge: Boydell & Brewer.

Swanwick, K. (1994) *Musical Knowledge: Intuition, Analysis and Music Education*. London: RoutledgeFalmer.

## Websites

www.education.gov.uk
www.ks2music.org.uk
www.singup.org

# Part 2

# Access and inclusion
## Setting the scene

*Gary Spruce*

The Wider Opportunities Pledge that 'Over time, all pupils in primary schools who wish to will have the opportunity to learn a musical instrument'[1] represents a unique commitment by a United Kingdom government to the principle of all children having access to an aspect of music education that hitherto has been available to only a minority. However, despite the fact that in educational discourse the terms are commonly linked, *access* does not necessarily or inevitably result in *inclusion*. One might argue that, whilst the Wider Opportunities Pledge, and the model of whole class instrumental and vocal teaching (WCIVT) that has emerged from it, go a long way to addressing the issue of access, neither addresses as a matter of course the more challenging aspect of inclusion. In this section we consider the issue of access and, particularly, inclusion in WCIVT from a range of perspectives.

When asked to define the implications of the principle of access and inclusion, respondents might include ensuring that all children have access to, and are included in, a curriculum which is appropriate to their needs, and that barriers to such access and inclusion are addressed. These barriers might then be identified as relating to cognitive or behavioural difficulties and physical impairments. Addressing such barriers is clearly important, but only partially meets the challenge raised by our commitment as teachers to ensuring that all children have not only access to a curriculum, but that they are also included in it. For one might argue that the story of universal access to education by children (in Western society) over the last hundred or so years is also the story of many children's alienation *from it* through their lack of inclusion *in it*.

This lack of inclusion is often the consequence of formal education (that which takes place in school) reflecting through its curriculum, assessment and pedagogy the values and norms of dominant social, religious, gender and cultural groupings which children often find alienating or irrelevant. When children perceive these values and norms as rejecting and devaluing what they consider to be important and relevant, or do not recognise them as reflecting their understanding of their world, then alienation from formal education occurs. This has been particularly the case in music where, until relatively recently, the exclusive promotion of the practices of 'classical' music, which reflect particular cultural and social values, saw many children reject school music. This resulted in the deep irony of the subject that many children engage with most out of school being one of the least popular on the curriculum (Harland *et al.* 2000).

It follows from this that if the inclusion aim of WCIVT and the Wider Opportunities Pledge is to be realised, then teachers need to adopt a broad approach. This approach needs to focus not only on addressing those barriers to learning that are presented through cognitive, behavioural and physical needs and impairments (what one might call classic special education needs) but also those barriers that result from the promotion of musical values and norms which children are unable to relate to and which they perceive as failing to reflect, or have the potential to project, their musical identities.

In seeking a vision for access and inclusion one might agree with Jellison (2006: 257) when she writes that 'The challenge for music education is to provide appropriate opportunities for all children in a variety of educational and social settings, so that children will participate happily and successfully in quality musical experiences', but that the strategies and processes for doing this must, in the words of Lucy Green, 'centre around the importance of listening to young people's voices and taking their values and their culture seriously' (Green 2008: 185).

In this section, four authors consider access and inclusion from a range of perspectives. In the first chapter, 'The developing musician', Lis McCullough identifies two issues that recur throughout the book. First, if teachers are to provide for children's musical needs, then they need to *know their children as musicians*. However, in order to come to this knowing, teachers need to understand what is meant by musical achievement and development, the many ways in which children demonstrate such achievement and development and the factors that impact upon it. Without this understanding, teachers cannot hope to really understand what it is that they are trying to achieve, be able to engage in musical discourse with their pupils and consequently address issues of access and inclusion.

Recognition of the diverse ways in which children demonstrate musical development (knowledge, understanding and skills) is central to the challenge of access and inclusion. For, if one aspect of musical development (e.g. performing) is promoted in music rooms to the exclusion or near exclusion of others, then not only is children's musical experience impoverished but those children who demonstrate musical development and achievement in another unexplored area can be seen as failing.

The second issue identified by McCullough is the importance of children trusting that the musical skills, understanding and values that they bring to the music classroom are appreciated and respected, and that links will be made between their musical lives in and out of school. Without this respect and without such links there is a danger that they will feel excluded from the music curriculum and suffer alienation from it.

Teaching large groups of children can be a concern for those teachers whose prior experience has been with individuals and small groups. Sometimes this results in teaching which focuses on 'managing children' rather than teaching them. In the second chapter, 'Promoting an inclusive music classroom', Carolyn Cooke makes the point that the best way of addressing or pre-empting challenging behaviour is through teaching which is underpinned by the principle of access and inclusion and a commitment by teachers to coming to know those they teach. She then goes on to develop the case for making the musical values and skills which children bring to school the starting point for creating a music classroom in which all feel included. She argues that children are most likely to experience a sense of inclusion and consequently remain engaged with their learning 'when they are in a state of complete absorption in the task – when they have achieved a state of "flow"'. Drawing on the work of Nakamura and Csikszentmihalyi (2002), she describes how the factors that contribute to achieving this state of flow might be achieved within the classroom.

It is evident therefore that the most important factor in ensuring that children feel included in the music classroom is ensuring that their musical lives outside the classroom, and the musical values and skills that are developed in these lives, are treated with respect, and are valued and celebrated within the classroom. This respect for the children as autonomous musicians is fundamental to inclusion and to supporting them in exploring what Katherine Zeserson in 'Musical styles, genres and traditions: creating a global musical heritage' describes as the 'vast richness of our global heritage'. She makes the critical point that the range of musical practices that are exhibited within different musical styles, genres and cultures 'offer a wide range of entry points to musical learning' for all children and 'are therefore powerfully inclusive classroom tools'. In a chapter that draws on a wide range of musical examples she demonstrates how, within whole class instrumental and vocal lessons, teachers can 'present a wide range of musical territories [for children and teachers] to navigate together and discoveries to share'.

In the final chapter of this section, 'Including those with special educational needs: "whole" class instrumental and vocal teaching', Sally Zimmermann argues for an inclusive approach to meeting the needs of all children including those with special educational needs. Although outlining the characteristics presented by children with particular categories of special educational needs, she suggests that 'inclusion' in this context should be about making only those adjustments that are necessary to ensure these children are included. In a telling phrase she argues that we must avoid slipping into stereotypical assumptions about what particular needs require but rather to 'address pupils' difficulties, but only where observably necessary ... we teach the child not the label'. She contends that most children's needs can be met through strategies that characterise all good teaching.

Teaching strategies are, of course, as important, as is planning and drawing on a wide range of musical styles and traditions. However, maybe all of these simply contribute to one overarching aim, which is, in the words of Witchell (2001: 204), for music teaching to 'contribute to the humanity of all children so that its impact is sustained throughout their lives. That is a good aim for all schools and music teachers. It should also be our bottom line in ensuring that music in schools meets the individual needs of all pupils'.

## Note

1 The Wider Opportunities Pledge was given by David Blunkett, the then Secretary of State for Education, and applied only to schools in England.

## References

Green, L. (2008) *Music, Informal Learning and the School: A New Classroom Pedagogy*. Aldershot: Ashgate.

Harland, J., Kinder, K., Lord, P., Stott, A., Schagen, I. and Haynes, J. (2000) *Arts Education in Secondary Schools: Effects and Effectiveness*. Clough: National Federation for Educational Research.

Jellison, J. A. (2006) 'Including everyone', in G. McPherson (ed.) *The Child as Musician*. Oxford: Oxford University Press.

Nakamura, J. and Csikszentmihalyi, M. (2002) 'The concept of flow', in C. R. Snyder and S. Lopez (eds) *Handbook of Positive Psychology*. Oxford: Oxford University Press.

Witchell, J. (2001) 'Music education and individual needs', in C. Philpott and C. Plummeridge (eds) *Issues in Music Teaching*. London: RoutledgeFalmer.

# Chapter 3

# The developing musician

*Lis McCullough*

## Introduction

Knowledge about musical development is important because the decisions teachers make are determined by their underlying thoughts, beliefs and attitudes. Therefore, what teachers consider musical development to be underpins what and how they plan, teach, and evaluate what their pupils do. Theory underpins practice – consciously or not – but this is a two-way process since practical experience helps develop personal theories.

This chapter gives an overview of some of the current thinking about musical development and makes links to the implications for whole class instrumental and vocal teaching (WCIVT), covering the following aspects:

- the nature of musical development;
- some theories of development in musical and related fields;
- how aspects of musical development can be recognised in the classroom;
- how musical development can be supported.

## What do we mean by musical development?

In an educational context, development implies some sort of change for the better – however defined – over time. The terms 'development' and 'progression' are commonly used almost interchangeably, and can be thought of in a generalised, holistic way or within specific aspects relating to music.

Those different aspects of musical development include:

- the different types of musical knowledge: knowledge *how* (skills), knowledge *that* (facts about) and knowledge *of* (acquaintance knowledge). While the latter is the 'absolutely central core involved in knowing music' (Swanwick 1994: 17), the other two can be contributory. For example, facts about a particular piece of music can influence the listener's appreciation of it; and technical skills can enable people to compose and perform in the ways they want;
- different ways of engaging with music (e.g. composing, performing, listening, appraising, singing, notating);
- conceptual development relating to the building blocks within music itself (what the National Curriculum refers to as 'elements': pitch, duration, timbre, etc.).

However, just as music contributes to the development of the whole child (Welch and Adams 2003; Hallam 2009), so musical development is influenced by various extra-musical aspects such as physical, emotional and social development. For instance, a child's ability to sing in tune and to play a tambourine on the beat arguably owes as much to physical maturation and control as to concept development relating to pitch and rhythm.

Yet ultimately, although the subject can be broken down both in order to make sense of the notion of development and for practical teaching purposes, the aim is for holistic growth in understanding, skills and commitment that comprise music as 'a way of thinking, a way of knowing' (Swanwick 1999: 23).

---

*Activity 3.1 Thinking about musical development*

An experienced teacher unpicks what musical development means to her:

> I tried to think of all the words I would associate with musical development and the following came into my head – confidence, co-ordination, recognising, analysing, reporting, creating, development of a sense of rhythm, a sense of pitch, general skills in listening, performing and composing, and coming to see the connections between all of these.
>
> (Meyer and Lamont 2009: 44)

What comes into *your* head? Jot down as many words as possible and then try to group them in ways that make sense to you – perhaps beginning with some of the divisions earlier in the chapter. This will provide a useful checklist when:

- considering the development of the class as a whole, as well as of individuals;
- planning long-, medium- and short-term;
- reflecting on the effect of sessions and activities;
- talking to children about their learning.

---

## Some theories of musical development

Table 3.1 gives an overview of how some authors and documents depict development in music and related areas. These describe normative development, relating to most children most of the time, and there may well be exceptions as far as individual children are concerned. It should also be remembered that any ages given are inevitably only a rough guide. The continuum through to early adulthood is included to help place Key Stage 2 pupils within their musical journey.

From Table 3.1 it can be seen that there is 'no single or unanimous voice … but rather a rainbow of ideas and opinions' (McPherson 2006: v). Nevertheless there does seem to be a general overarching pattern of development from a pre-conventional, sensorimotor explora-tion of the basic materials of sound and sound maker (including the human music maker) to a conventional phase where a child recognises how music 'works': the patterns and norms that characterise it in whichever dominant culture(s) the child is raised. Key Stage 2 is the time when children can become intent on mastering the norms around them – think of the recorder player practising *London's Burning* almost incessantly! There is also some evidence that children are more 'open-eared' to a range of musical styles at this stage than in adolescence (see Hargreaves 1996: 164). Having learnt the 'rules' of the immediate musical cultures (through enculturation as well as instruction), young people may move on to 'breaking' and playing with them, before passing on to a post-conventional phase where they can take a more reflective perspective both of music in general and of their own specific and individualised commitment. Similar progression is also found in moral and social development as well as in other arts' fields and in language development.

## How can children's musical development be recognised?

As it is not possible to *see* what a child thinks, it is necessary to watch as well as listen to what children do and say, and compare that across time – a term, a year, a key stage. Ofsted recommends building up a bank of recorded examples within a school not only as a way of keeping records of children/classes but also 'to develop a shared understanding of expectations about progress for each year group' (2009: 18). However, because of the range of aspects involved, one should remember that:

- a child who cannot explain what s/he is doing does not necessarily lack understanding of the related concepts;
- an articulate child with appropriate terminology may not be able to put that knowledge into practice;
- attitudes and physical skills play an important role in what a child can and does do;
- there may be variation within individuals. For example, a child with advanced technical skills when playing a notated piece on an instrument may not be so confident when composing;
- children may seem to regress in unfamiliar situations.

Considering children's actual music making is, of course, crucial to teachers' understanding of their pupils' understanding. However, it is also possible to use more tangential methods by, for instance, providing opportunities to represent music in other art forms, such as dance.

Graphic notation is another valuable way of facilitating teachers' access to pupils' musical thinking and development, while also being an important means of:

- 'storing' music so it can be recalled at another time;
- enabling pupils to make connections between sonic and visual media;
- providing a way in to traditional staff notation.

Jeanne Bamberger's research (see Table 3.1) relates particularly to rhythm and melody, and in a freer situation other aspects may also be observed. For example, after the scribbling (enactive) phase, there may then be a representative (iconic) phase where either the instrument or the person playing it is the focus, before a graphic (symbolic) phase is reached. Although the exact conventions relating to formal staff notation need to be learnt, individual aspects of such notation, for example pairs of quavers, often occur symbolically in children's own notations because they are exposed to such images in their everyday lives.

Table 3.1 Comparing views of development

| Authors and brief description | Ages and titles of phases (if given) | | | |
|---|---|---|---|---|
| **Swanwick and Tillman (1986)** Relates to composing, but since used for listening/appraising and performing. Draws on Piaget (1951). Cumulative – previous levels subsumed in latter. | **0–4 Materials** Exploration of materials of sound and sound makers. Fascination with sound quality – both timbre and the extremes of pitch, dynamics and duration – plus physical manipulation of sound makers, seen in exploration of instruments and voice, e.g. up and down xylophone bars. Compositions often rambling. | **4–9 Expression** Music as expressive character, through changes in, especially, speed and dynamics. Apparent lack of structural control gives way to short gestures/phrases, which become more conventional in length and structure by age 7/8. | **10–15 Form** Vernacular of surrounding culture firmly established, allowing for experiment and surprise. Recognition and use of repetition, transformation, contrast and links. 'Technical, expressive and structural control begins to be established reliably over longer periods of time' (333). Popular music influential. | **15+ Value** 'Awareness of the personal and cultural *value* of music: shown in autonomy, independent critical evaluation and sustained commitment to specific musical styles' (Swanwick 1999: 81). |
| **Parsons (1987)** Based on visual arts (Piaget-type stage theory) but with implications across other arts. No ages suggested after the first stage because dependent on experience. | **0–5 Favouritism** Child attracted by colour and subject as they relate to and therefore appeal to her/him. | **Beauty and realism** Beauty, realism and technical skill are important. | **Expressiveness** Emotional power of a painting important; understanding the 'message', based on personal experience. Aware others have different views. | **Style and form** Concern with the form and style of a painting, especially in relation to its social context/tradition. **Autonomy** Reflective attitude towards value of individual art works in cultural context, weighing one's own views against others'. |

Table 3.1  Continued

| Authors and brief description | Ages and titles of phases (if given) | | | | |
|---|---|---|---|---|---|
| **Gardner (1973/1994)** 'Symbol system' theory of artistic development developed within Harvard Project Zero. Three interlocking systems of feeling, perceiving and making. | **0–1 Pre-symbolic period** (cannot conceive of what is not present). Sensorimotor, 'unfolding' and exploration of the three systems. | **1–7 Period of symbol use** Gaining necessary experiences and skills to take part in artistic processes. Beginning to acquire conventions of artistic processes and products. Domain specific – music is a unique symbol system. | **7+ Later artistic development** Increase in skills and use of symbols, critical judgement and reflective thought. | | |
| **Welch (2006)** **Moog (1976)** Vocal/song development. | **0–2** Babbling and vocal play leads to outline and partial songs, often repetitious. Individual pitches and melodic contour, but lack of overall coherence and inconsistent rhythm and sense of tonality (home note). | **2–4** Pot-pourri songs where own spontaneous songs borrow aspects from known songs. Global outline songs with more rhythmic organisation and recognisable melodic contour. | **4–8** New songs usually learnt in following order: words, rhythm, melodic contour, specific intervals. Pitching stabilises – individual notes, then melodic contour, smaller melodic fragments, whole song. Own songs show known conventions, e.g. structure and emotional expression. | **8–11** Most children singing in tune by the age of 11, though boys tend to lag behind girls. Can sustain longer phrases. Finer control of dynamics and rhythm. | **11–15** Changes in voice due to physical development usually 12–14, but can be as young as 8/9: breathiness in girls, reduced vocal range and pitch stability in boys. |

| Authors and brief description | Ages and titles of phases (if given) | | | |
| --- | --- | --- | --- | --- |
| **Bamberger (1991, 2006)** Explores how graphic representations of music reveal how children understand music, particularly rhythm and pitch. NB. Types F and M are interactive rather than independent and sequential. | **Type O** Pre-representational 'rhythmic scribbles' corresponding to music's movement. | **Type F – Figural** Based on how the individual 'chunks' the music, i.e. the 'shapes' perceived within the music and the function of individual sounds within those groups, and the dominant features, e.g. the loudness of a particular note/section. More intuitive (e.g. 'slow slow quick quick slow, slow slow quick quick slow' represented as two long/large notes and then three short/small, repeated). | **Type M – Metric** Context-independent groupings of sounds (long long short short long) with regular/consistent divisions of time. Both metric and figural representations develop over time as children's perceptions and strategies develop. In both types, children likely to include more than one dimension as they become older, e.g. rhythm and dynamics. | **(Formal staff notation)** (A result of tuition rather than intuition.) |
| **National Curriculum** (England) First sentences from level descriptions (DfEE/QCA 1999: 36–37). (KS sections: 'Expected attainment for the majority of pupils at the end of the key stage', with the 'great majority' working within levels in brackets under KS heading.) | **KS1** (levels 1–3) Level 1: 'Pupils recognise and explore how sounds can be made and changed.' Level 2: 'Pupils recognise and explore how sounds can be organised.' | **KS2** (levels 2–5) Level 3: 'Pupils recognise and explore the ways sounds can be combined and used expressively.' Level 4: 'Pupils identify and explore the relationship between sounds and how music reflects different intentions.' | **KS3** (levels 3–7) Level 5: 'Pupils identify and explore musical devices and how music reflects time and place.' Level 6: 'Pupils identify and explore the different processes and contexts of selected musical genres and styles.' | Level 7: 'Pupils discriminate and explore musical conventions in, and influences on, selected genres, styles and traditions.' Level 8: 'Pupils discriminate and exploit the characteristics and expressive potential of selected musical resources, genres, styles and traditions.' Exceptional performance: 'Pupils discriminate and develop different interpretations. They express their own ideas and feelings in a developing personal style …'. |

*Activity 3.2 Using graphic notation to investigate musical development*

Plan an activity in which children use their own graphic notation to represent part of a piece they have learnt to play/sing. When they have done this, look at their work and consider the following questions:

- What do the representations show you about how the children are thinking?
- What aspects are being represented? What aspects are not?
- How many aspects are included at any one time?

Carry out a similar activity during the following term. Can you see any changes indicating a development in specific pupils' thinking about (any aspect of) music?

Think about how you could use their notations to help develop children's thinking, perhaps in relation to pitch – a notoriously tricky concept to understand, not least because of the terminology used. Could you use the notation in constructive ways in future sessions, maybe by suggesting pupils compose a piece based on someone else's notation? This would not only help them consider what aspects of music can be notated and how they can be interpreted, but would also underline the main purpose of notation: to store music in a way that can be read not only by the composer, but also by others.

## Implications for the whole class instrumental and vocal teaching classroom

Modern cognitive psychology holds that we learn by constructing our own knowledge, based on the experiences we have. This knowledge builds on previous knowledge, and then itself becomes the basis for further new knowledge. The more ways in which different aspects can be linked up, the more rounded will become the concepts held. Not only does this imply new learning needs to be based on existing knowledge, but it also underlines the importance of breadth of experience. It has, for instance, been suggested that an effective WCIVT programme might accelerate pupils through the Swanwick/Tillman levels (Stafford 2009).

Because of the range of individuals' background experiences and the many aspects involved in musical development, children in a Wider Opportunities class will be at different stages of development and therefore teachers need activities that can accommodate different levels of physical control and musical understanding, while giving opportunities for growth. During childhood, practical engagement is vital to the formation of mental concepts. The following case study shows how one teacher devised an activity for consolidation and practice of existing knowledge ('that', 'how' and 'of'), while giving opportunities for individuals to extend their thinking – especially in relation to pitch, rhythm and structure – through improvisation and performance.

*Case study: A multi-functional resource*

A cornet teacher prepares for a session with Year 4 children and their class teacher by using the loop facility on GarageBand (software free with Macs) to construct a backing track. She teaches the class a simple rap based on the names of the parts of the cornet and uses the backing track as accompaniment.

Still using the backing track, she plays a two-bar, eight-beat tune on her cornet using the two notes that the children already know and encourages them to join in when ready. That tune, with everyone playing, is then used as the A section of a rondo piece (structured ABACADA ...) where individual children take turns to improvise in the intervening (B, C, D ...) sections. The teacher provides an early section using just one note and a very simple rhythm – in order to ensure everyone has something within their technical grasp. In a later session she feeds in more sophisticated rhythmic ideas for those children who would benefit from being stretched.

This activity thus:

- allows individuals to respond at their own level;
- gives opportunities for the teachers to observe individuals' responses and support and extend as necessary;
- helps pupils benefit from others' responses;
- ensures even the simplest instrumental offerings sounds like 'real music', thus enhancing enjoyment and self-esteem.

In following sessions the instrumental teacher uses the backing track:

- in various warm ups, for example, using the rap; or where teacher and then pupils use body percussion to lead the rest of the class in simple ostinati;
- in call and response activities when learning new notes;
- as a basis for exploring different structures and styles.

The class teacher uses it for encouraging improvising with classroom percussion instruments. He also copies it onto CDs for pupils to use at home.

Some of the pupils investigate how they can access loops in Compose World and E Jay (computer software already owned by the school) to develop rhythm tracks, which they then use to accompany their own raps.

Children develop their knowledge of music and their self-identity as musicians from all their musical experiences – and so it is important to acknowledge and respect what a child brings from outside school. As with other areas of the curriculum, concrete experience is important at this stage. However, children, especially in the early years of KS2 or when facing new material, may find it difficult to focus on more than one aspect at a time, so that, for example, correct tuning may temporarily come at the expense of rhythmic accuracy, or vice versa.

As development in music is neither linear nor necessarily consistent across the various aspects, there are multiple ways of making progress. Children can play known pieces more musically, as well as playing longer, faster, more technically challenging ones. Musical development can be encouraged through the breadth of curriculum, challenge within activities and quality of the outcome. This does not necessarily mean doing different things, since similar concepts and activities can be tackled in different contexts, or extra components can be added to something known.

---

*Activity 3.3 Planning for musical development*

Plan a unit of work (between four weeks and half a term in length). Show clearly:

- how this builds on your pupils' previous experiences;
- the planned steps to promote conceptual and/or physical progression within this aspect;
- how and when differentiation is allowed for.

Choose one particular aspect of musical development (e.g. performing or an element such as rhythm) and identify when and how you will identify and record development in this area. Although you may, of course, also see other aspects when actually teaching this unit, it is helpful to include a specific focus when planning so that you can:

- build in specific points when you concentrate on one aspect (trying to do everything at once is impossible!);
- cover a range of different aspects over a series of units of work.

---

## Conclusion

This chapter has demonstrated how musical development is complex and multi-faceted, comprised of both musical and extra-musical aspects, and that there is no one way of describing what is thus a matrix-like profile of progression. However, this also gives potential for a correspondingly broad range of learning opportunities within which individuals can acquire and demonstrate understanding across the breadth of aspects that contribute to holistic musicality, in a range of ways that cater for different preferences and learning styles.

Children's development is influenced by all their experiences – intentionally or not. There is, for example, anecdotal evidence that previous experience of the national singing programme Sing Up initiative enhances pupils' rhythmic response at the start of WCIVT programmes. Proposed changes to the primary curriculum (Rose 2009) suggested exciting opportunities for making deep-level links between different subjects – both within the arts and across areas of learning – thus enhancing concepts relating to all subjects, while retaining the essential natures of individual ones.

Musical development is lifelong. Therefore not only are teachers contributing to their pupils' future engagement with music but they are also participating in their own musical journeys. The educationalist John Holt (1978/1991) told the tale of his own musical life story in a fascinating book entitled *Never Too Late* – words to encourage any teacher involved in a WCIVT programme.

# References

Bamberger, J. (1991) *The Mind behind the Musical Ear: How Children Develop Musical Intelligence.* Cambridge, MA: Harvard University Press.

Bamberger, J. (2006) 'What develops in musical development?', in G. E. McPherson (ed.) *The Child as Musician: A Handbook of Musical Development.* New York: Oxford University Press.

Coll, H. and Lamont, A. (eds) (2009) *Sound Progress: Exploring Musical Development.* Matlock: National Association of Music Educators. Available from www.name.org.uk.

Department for Education and Employment/Qualifications and Curriculum Authority (DfEE/QCA) (1999) *Music.* London: HMSO.

Gardner, H. (1973/1994) *The Arts and Human Development.* New York: John Wiley.

Hallam, S. (2009) *The Power of Music: Its Impact on the Intellectual, Social and Personal Development of Children and Young People.* Downloadable free from www.ioe.ac.uk/Year_of_Music.pdf (accessed Oct. 2009).

Hargreaves, D. (1996) 'The development of artistic and musical competence', in I. DeLiege and J. A. Sloboda (eds) *Musical Beginnings: Origins and Development of Musical Competence.* Oxford: Oxford University Press.

Holt, J. (1978/1991) *Never Too Late: My Musical Life Story.* Cambridge, Massachusetts: Perseus Books.

McPherson, G. E. (ed.) (2006) *The Child as Musician: A Handbook of Musical Development.* New York: Oxford University Press.

Meyer, H. and Lamont, A. (2009) 'Musical development at Key Stage 3', in H. Coll and A. Lamont (eds) *Sound Progress: Exploring Musical Development.* Matlock: National Association of Music Educators.

Mills, J. (2009) *Music in the Primary School* (3rd edn). Oxford: Oxford University Press.

Moog, H. (1976) *The Musical Experience of the Pre-School Child.* London: Schott.

Ofsted (2009) *Making More of Music: An Evaluation of Music in Schools 2005/08.* London: Ofsted. Downloadable free from www.ofsted.gov.uk (accessed Oct. 2009).

Parsons, M. J. (1987) *How We Understand Art.* Cambridge: Cambridge University Press.

Piaget, J. (1951) *Play, Dreams and Imitation in Childhood.* London: Heinemann.

Rose, J. (2009) *Independent Review of the Primary Curriculum: Final Report.* London: DCSF.

Stafford, E. (2009) 'Whole class instrumental and vocal teaching: A catalyst for musical development?', in H. Coll and A. Lamont (eds) *Sound Progress: Exploring Musical Development.* Matlock: National Association of Music Educators.

Swanwick, K. (1994) *Musical Knowledge: Intuition, Analysis and Music Education.* London: Routledge.

Swanwick, K. (1999) *Teaching Music Musically.* London: Routledge.

Swanwick, K. and Tillman, J. (1986) 'The sequence of musical development: A study of children's composition', *British Journal of Music Education*, 3(3): 305–339.

Welch, G. F. (2006) 'Singing and vocal development', in G. E. McPherson (ed.) *The Child as Musician: A Handbook of Musical Development.* New York: Oxford University Press.

Welch, G. F. and Adams, P. (2003) *How is Music Learning Celebrated and Developed?* Southwell, Notts: BERA. Downloadable free from www.bera.ac.uk/files/2008/09/musicp1.pdf (accessed Oct. 2009).

## Further reading

*How is Music Learning Celebrated and Developed?* (Welch and Adams 2003) – a user-friendly free download drawing out practical implications from research.

*Music in the Primary School* (Mills 2009, 3rd edn) – a key handbook for anyone working in primary schools.

*Sound Progress: Exploring Musical Development* (Coll and Lamont 2009) – a compilation from practitioners across the music education spectrum.

*The Child as Musician: A Handbook of Musical Development* (McPherson 2006) – a comprehensive academic work for those who want to read more deeply about research in this area.

# Chapter 4

# Promoting an inclusive music classroom

*Carolyn Cooke*

## Introduction

Providing for the needs of large groups of children can present significant challenges for teachers, particularly if their experience hitherto has been primarily teaching individuals or small groups. Teachers' fears about 'classroom management' and the assumption that controlling children is separate in some way from teaching them can lead them to seek out techniques or tricks for guaranteeing good behaviour. However, as Chris Philpott says, this 'is a fallacy, for it is through effective learning and teaching in music that pupils can be inspired to behave well' (Philpott in Philpott and Spruce 2007: 102).

At the very heart of the Wider Opportunities Programme (whole class instrumental and vocal teaching – WCIVT) is a fundamental belief that a high quality musical education should be made available to all. Creating an inclusive musical experience that not only develops pupils' musicality but also inspires them is key to ensuring that children engage and remain engaged with their music making and music learning.

A commitment to achieving an inclusive environment requires of teachers one thing above all others: that they develop and maintain a rich and sophisticated relationship with, and knowledge of, their pupils. This knowledge might include their levels of achievement and special educational or behavioural needs, including being gifted and talented. Above all, however, it will require knowledge of pupils as *musicians*, including not only their instrumental and vocal skills but also the musical cultures they are part of and the musical activities that they are involved in both in and out of school. It is only through developing and then using this knowledge that teachers can plan lessons that will fully engage all pupils in rich and personally meaningful musical learning.

Successful inclusion occurs when teachers use knowledge of their pupils to:

- personalise pupils' musical learning;
- provide engaging musical encounters for all pupils;
- create and manage the environment so that all pupils are able to learn effectively.

It is at the point where these three aspects meet that the most effective inclusion takes place (see Figure 4.1).

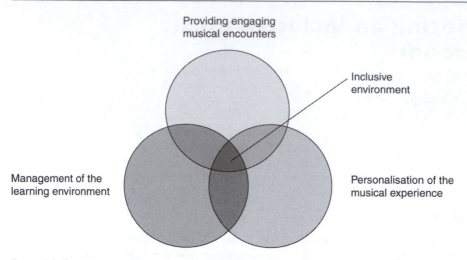

*Figure 4.1* Creating an inclusive musical environment

In this chapter we are going to look in detail at these three aspects and consider strategies for bringing them about.

## Promoting inclusivity through *personalisation*

Personalisation within a whole class teaching scenario can seem a daunting, and sometimes unmanageable, aim. However, personalisation does not mean different lessons or resources for every child but, rather, understanding that individual pupils can gain different learning experiences through carefully planned lessons. In this way personalisation can be seen as twofold: how the pupil experiences and perceives their role in the lesson, and how the teacher can use personalisation as a strategy to inform future planning.

### *Knowing your pupils as musicians*

Pupils will bring to their learning a broad and constantly developing range of musical experiences and knowledge. Taking account of this experience and knowledge helps maintain an effective balance between stretching individual pupils and making tasks achievable. From a pupil's perspective, acknowledgement of prior learning is critical to how they will respond to, and therefore learn from, the music session. Therefore, finding out about pupils should take place at an early stage and be a continuous process (see Figure 4.2).

Discussions between teachers and other adults who have a working knowledge of the pupils is a crucial starting point. In the context of Wider Opportunity Programmes (WCIVT), discussion between all those involved in the teaching – and particularly between the class teacher and instrumental tutor – is critical. Such discussions need to continue after the lesson to include evaluations of the effectiveness of teaching, the progress made by individuals and groups of pupils and deciding 'where next'.

*Whole class:*

- What music has the class participated in (genres/styles/activities/performances)?
- Are there regular routines, games or songs that the class are used to in their music lessons or daily routines?
- What instruments have the class had prior access to? In what context were they used?
- What musical language/notation systems are they familiar with?

*Groups within the class:*

- Are there groups within this class who have had additional musical experience through extra-curricular work or one-off experiences? What were they and who was involved?
- Has this led to a different range of instrumental, vocal or composition skills from therest of the class?
- Do they have experience of a broader musical vocabulary/use of notation?

*Individuals:*

- Which individuals are musically active outside of the curriculum? What is it they areinvolved in
  (culture, type of group, instruments, repertoire, style of learning)?
- Who has had instrumental or vocal lessons (including pupils who have stopped having them)?
- What musical understanding is going to be directly transferable to the whole class teaching situation or how can the planning create opportunities for transferring understanding?

*Figure 4.2* Knowing your pupils as musicians: a starting point for building personalisation

### Individual needs

Some pupils need more individualised planning. This may be because they have additional musical experience, because they have a physical or emotional need that needs addressing, or it may be because they need additional support with an aspect of musical development. Successfully planning for such individuals relies heavily on how well you know the pupils' needs, and how you interact with the pupil during the lessons to deepen your knowledge of their abilities to inform future planning. Planning support for pupils based on this knowledge and then enacting this support in a way that allows the pupils to experience a meaningful musical experience is fundamental to personalising learning.

In the case study below we look at how a personalised approach to learning is used to support pupils identified as musically gifted and talented.

*Case study: A whole class ukulele programme*

A teacher running a ukulele programme makes specific reference in her planning to two pupils who have additional musical experience, a pianist and a cellist. She plans lessons that enable them both to explore a variety of roles, such as leading a call and response and maintaining an individual part within a small group. Within the scheme she draws on the pianist's knowledge of notated chords, and extends his knowledge by helping him relate this to chord symbols. The cellist's knowledge of string instruments and fingering enables the teacher to help him explore sound quality and dynamics at an earlier stage while extending the range of chords and picking patterns he can use. As well as providing objectives and opportunities to both pupils, the teacher communicates at an appropriate level with them by tailoring the questions she asks, the musical vocabulary she uses and the type of musical response she praises them for. Although the planning and delivery for these pupils is personalised, it is within the context of the same musical experience that the whole class is involved in.

In lessons which focus primarily on instrumental learning there is a danger that only those children with particular instrumental performing skills are recognised as gifted and talented. Children will demonstrate particular musical talent in a range of ways, for example through having particularly acute powers of musical recall or sensitivity to musical timbre, pitch or rhythm which might be demonstrated through improvising or composing activities. It is critical therefore that if such children are to be fully included in WCIVT lessons there are opportunities for them to demonstrate their talents so that the teacher can plan for and support their further development.

*Activity 4.1 Gifted and talented pupils*

Identify two children who you teach in whole class instrumental classes who might be considered to be musically gifted and talented, one in performing and the other in composing or improvising. For each one:

- identify exactly the musical skills and understanding that you feel makes them gifted and talented;
- Identify ways in which you will plan opportunities for them to demonstrate and extend their particular skills and understanding within the whole class context.

## Personalised interactions

As has been established, it is necessary to identify individual achievement, progress and any barriers to learning (cultural, physical, cognitive or behavioural) in order to plan effectively for musical learning which promotes inclusion. In whole class settings it is particularly important that all pupils feel that they can make a significant individual musical contribution. To identify what this contribution might be, interactions with pupils during a lesson need to include personal interactions. By personal interactions we mean ones that are based on musical knowledge of the individual child and are directed to meeting their specific musical needs and ensuring that these are met through enabling them to contribute. By personalising the interactions, rather than speaking generically to the class or groups of pupils all the time, the pupil not only receives relevant and appropriate support and feedback but also has greater sense of control over their learning. The potential impact of such personalised interactions is outlined in Figure 4.3.

| Personal interactions | Outcomes for promoting inclusivity |
|---|---|
| Recognising individual achievement | Pupils are motivated to succeed and stay on task. Pupils know their contribution is important to the overall musical experience. Pupils are aware that praise and personal interaction will result from engagement with the musical learning. |
| Recognising pupil progress | Pupils are motivated to succeed and stay on task. Pupils are aware of the progress they have made both towards the objectives and towards unplanned learning outcomes, making progress more holistic by accounting for all types of learning and outcomes. |
| Recognising difficulties in accessing the learning | Pupils feel supported in their learning. Pupils know that you will spend the necessary time, or modify the activity, to help them to participate and engage fully as part of the class. Pupils are aware that overcoming difficulties with your help will lead to recognition of their progress and achievements which reinforces their motivation and engagement. |

Figure 4.3 Personalisation and inclusivity

*Activity 4.2 Identifying prior musical experiences as the basis
            for personalisation*

Choose a class and a particular lesson that you are going to teach. Select four individuals from that class who have a range of musical experiences and then:

- using Figure 4.2 identify, if appropriate through discussion with other teachers, the children's prior musical experiences;
- using Figure 4.2 consider how you will use this information to provide a personalised experience for them during a particular lesson;
- design a set of five questions to ask the four pupils after the lesson to help you evaluate how they responded to the strategies and the overall learning objectives.

## Promoting inclusivity by providing *engaging musical encounters*

Maintaining the interest and hence engagement of pupils in their musical learning is one of the most effective methods of ensuring inclusion and also of managing pupil behaviour. Key to achieving this engagement is creating an environment which constantly promotes rich and meaningful musical activity and experience. Finding creative ways to use music for different sections of the lesson and minimising the amount of time spent talking about, rather than engaging in, music can help achieve this aim. This might include setting the atmosphere on arrival by playing music that the pupils can join in with as soon as they have entered the room such as a song, an ostinato pattern that they have previously learnt, or a call and response activity. Using musical modelling (either by the teacher or pupils) to explain tasks and activities rather than describing what to do also helps maintain the musical experience. It is also possible to use non-verbal communication (such as hand gestures or physical presence) to moderate pupils' behaviour during musical activities rather than interrupting the flow of the lesson.

Another key element in maintaining engagement is to ensure that the lesson has sufficient 'light and shade': sections of the lesson that are fast paced and enable significant progress through many short activities whilst other parts create the space to allow pupils to engage with the musical experience and learning on a deeper level.

*Activity 4.3 Using music throughout the lesson*

Consider ways in which you might use music in the context of:

- pupils entering the space;
- taking a register;
- tuning up or warming up their instruments or bodies;
- dismissing the class in an orderly fashion.

Having established the importance of creating a musical environment it is now essential to consider strategies for providing an optimal musical learning experience.

Csikszentmihalyi (2002) suggests that people learn best when they are in a state of complete absorption in the task – when they have achieved a state of 'flow'. He identifies nine factors in the achievement of such 'flow' (see Figure 4.4).

Let us consider now the potential implications of these factors for children's musical learning. First, for pupils to find the planned activities meaningful and intrinsically rewarding, what they are asked to do must focus on the full range of what it is to be musical and not just on instrumental or vocal skill development. This could mean something as simple as exploring dynamics and articulation and their impact on the piece. They also need to understand the relevance of the activities to the planned outcomes: to understand the objectives and the planned progression towards them so they can see the learning journey they are taking.

Second, pupils need to feel that what they are being asked to do is musically relevant developmentally, in relation to both prior and future learning and in relation to their past and present musical experiences in and out of school. It is far more likely that pupils will engage and lose self-conscious inhibitions within the whole class learning environment if they work with music that is appropriate for them and relates to their musical lives outside of school. This requires of the teacher an in-depth knowledge of their pupils and an ability to highlight connections between prior, current and future learning. The musical activities that are chosen might be structured using a model of continuity, development and change addressing both progression and musical experience (see Figure 4.5). Using this model, learning could start from musical pieces that the class already knows, whether through school or outside, or choosing a style or genre where links can be made to music of which they already have an understanding.

1  Clear goals that are understood and attainable but of a high level.

2  Concentration level is high with all pupils having the opportunity to focus and engage deeply with the experience.

3  A loss of the feeling of self-consciousness.

4  Distorted sense of time: a pupil's experience of time is altered.

5  Direct and immediate feedback so that a pupil's behaviour or actions can be adjusted immediately.

6  Balance between ability level and challenge (the activity is neither too easy nor too difficult).

7  A sense of personal control over the situation or activity.

8  The activity is intrinsically rewarding, leading to a high level of engagement.

9  Pupils become absorbed in the activity.

*Figure 4.4* Csikszentmihalyi's nine factors to achieve flow

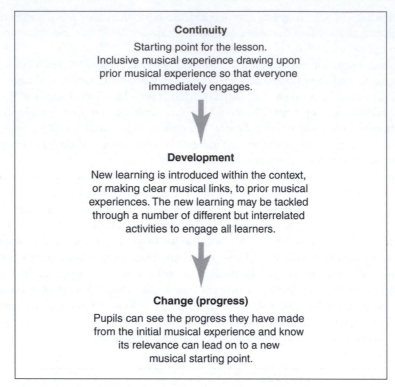

*Figure 4.5* Development and progression

---

*Activity 4.4 Demonstrating musical progression and development*

Using Figure 4.5 as a template, map out a whole class instrumental lesson which demonstrates development and progression. Show how in particular the lesson:

- builds on musical experience and learning that some of the children bring to their learning;
- introduces new learning and how this learning links to prior learning and experience;
- how you enable pupils to recognise the musical progress that they have made.

---

Third, the music selected should provide a range of experiences that are motivating and accessible for the whole class. Csikszentmihalyi states that to achieve optimal learning pupils should be given 'perceived challenges, or opportunities for action, that stretch (neither overmatching nor underutilizing) existing skills' (Nakamura and Csikszentmihalyi 2002). In creating an inclusive environment this will involve drawing on music that will develop and extend the children's musical experiences and meet the learning objectives whilst at the same time providing opportunity for achievement amongst all pupils. It is critical that the music chosen is of high quality and technically accessible so as to achieve a high level of engagement amongst pupils.

*Case study: A whole class violin lesson*

A violin group in their first weeks are exploring the A and D strings as part of a project where the children are exploring the musical style of the 'Hoedown' through listening, composing and performing. The starter activity of this lesson introduced the idea of drone and links are made between the tone quality the pupils are producing and the nature of the Hoedown as a dance. Some pupils experiment with playing both strings simultaneously and some have attempted using dynamic to create a dance feel. The teacher introduces a piece which uses an ostinato using A and D and divides the class in two, playing the rhythm on one note each. As soon as this is established, with the melody being played over the top by the teacher, the class is then divided into two groups: some maintain the rhythm while playing individual notes and others sustain both notes together. While modelling the task, the teacher adds dynamics and continues to draw attention to the tone quality. The pupils involved in each group are changed and rotated by the teacher, but any of the pupils can decide to try out the dynamics by watching the teacher when they feel ready. By the end of the lesson, all pupils have explored the idea of drone as well as experimenting with different bowing and articulation. As a class they organise a structure for playing the piece with these different elements.

---

*Activity 4.5 Choosing effective musical stimuli*

Consider how a piece of music that you have used or are planning to use in your teaching will:

- be of relevance to your pupils culturally and developmentally;
- provide all pupils with a rich musical experience;
- support the development of musical understanding.

---

## Promoting inclusivity through *managing the learning environment*

Every teaching environment is different and every class and individual within the class responds to the environment in different ways. Predicting and managing how the environment is going to impact on pupils' learning experience makes it far more likely that pupils will engage with the musical learning. By learning environment we mean not only the location but also the resources available to the pupils and the way the space is managed. It is important to negotiate a suitable space to enable musical learning to take place effectively. This may involve drawing up a case to present to the headteacher as to why a particular space is not only appropriate but necessary for the particular activities.

Pupils' association with a particular environment and their response to it can be very strong (e.g. school hall is associated with assemblies where they enter in silence and sit on the floor in a straight row). Music lessons are a unique moment in the school week and therefore require an association of their own so that pupils recognise the differences in the interactions they are expected to have. The key question to ask is, what tells pupils that this is the time to engage with learning and each other in a different way to other parts of their day? Musical-welcome strategies and starter routines can be particularly important in this respect and these can counteract the associations that pupils have with a particular location and immediately distinguish the lesson from previous learning. Equally, arrangement of the space, pupils and resources can provide a visual reminder that this time is different from other times.

---

**Case study: Teaching in the school hall**

A whole class flute group have their session in the school hall where they have their PE sessions (where they enter and immediately start to jog around the space) and assembly (where they enter in silence in lines). The class and music teacher have discussed how to establish the musical environment by using a Calypso song the class already knows. The song has space to sing hello to everyone in turn. The teachers use the song for the first few weeks and then start to adapt it to welcome each pupil, not by name but by asking them to respond with a short phrase on the flute. After a few more weeks the pupils have composed their own response to the welcome. This strategy announces the session as musical, engages everyone immediately in a musical activity, has room to adapt, extend and develop pupils' musical abilities and provides a personalised musical welcome.

---

One of the strongest visual reminders of the difference in expectations for a space can be the layout and where pupils are expected to stand or sit. Whereas a horseshoe or circle has a number of advantages from a management perspective, what is most important is that the configuration promotes a high quality and authentic musical experience. For example, for a vocal or drumming activity a circle might be more appropriate whereas a string group might emulate an orchestral layout. Gamelan or steel pans will require spatial organisation which reflects the cultural and performing tradition from which they derive.

Successful planning of the environment requires predicting potential barriers to learning. There are, however, instances where issues will arise which aren't as easy to predict such as unexpected changes to teaching spaces or the reaction of pupils to a distraction. When such distractions occur, the teacher needs to ask what actions (such as moving some pupils) might be taken to minimise or remove the distraction without causing pupils to become (further) disengaged from their musical learning.

---

**Case study: Re-establishing musical engagement**

Three children have become distracted by movement in a corridor. The class is involved in rhythmic call and response where the teacher has asked pupils to improvise two-bar rhythms. The teacher has already asked the three children to lead a call and response pattern but this has had limited success in re-engaging the pupils' attention. The teacher decides to move the activity on by having a group of pupils clapping a rhythmic pattern against which the call and response can take place. He uses the opportunity to move the three pupils to join others to form a backing group. This has the desired effect as the pupils re-engage with a sustained musical role and a different position in the class layout without interrupting the whole class engagement with the music. Equally the teacher hasn't verbally highlighted the distraction which may have led to more pupils being distracted by it. Having re-engaged the pupils, the teacher later switches the roles again so they participate fully in the call and response patterns.

The checklist (Figure 4.6) highlights some questions to ask when planning for an inclusive learning environment.

---

*Does the organisation of the space allow for:*

- musical interaction and eye contact between yourselves and all of the pupils?
- physical access to all pupils while still maintaining the musical experience with the rest of the class?
- assisting individual pupils or groups of pupils?
- maintaining engagement in the musical activities? Have steps been taken to minimise distractions from the windows, corridors, etc.?
- easy movement around the space? Has furniture or equipment been moved to allow this to happen?
- immediate engagement in musical activities? Is the space set up and ready to use from the first minute of the lesson?

*Are the pupils stood or sat in such a way that allows for:*

- every child to feel an integrated part of the whole class musical experience?
- smooth transitions between individual, small group and whole class interactions without moving large numbers of pupils?
- individuals or groups who will need additional supprt to be within close proximity of help?
- the full use of their instruments or voices? Have they all got enough room?
- all pupils to respond to instructions (whether spoken, sung, played or visual)?

*Are the resources organised and prepared to allow for:*

- immediate engagement in musical activities? Are the resources all ready to use from the start of the lesson?
- a clear routine for distributing, handling and putting away?
- every pupil to be able to access the resources for the lesson? Are there indiviudals who need resources adapting?

---

*Figure 4.6* Checklist for establishing an inclusive learning environment

## Conclusion

This chapter has established that an inclusive music classroom is characterised by a number of features. First, teachers knowing their pupils as musicians both in terms of the level of their musical understanding and skills but also their musical interests and aspirations and the knowledge that they bring to music lessons from their lives outside of school. Second, an inclusive classroom is a *musical* classroom where high quality musical experiences and learning are promoted as the key to maintaining pupils' engagement and interest in their learning in and beyond their WCIVT lessons. Third, inclusion does not just happen but needs to be planned for carefully. When these three characteristics occur then the conditions will be in place to ensure that the whole class instrumental lesson can meet the musical needs and aspirations of all children.

## References

Csikszentmihalyi, M. (2002) 'Foreword', in T. Sullivan and L. Willingham (eds) *Creativity and Music Education*. Toronto: Canadian Music Educators Association.

Nakamura, J. and Csikszentmihalyi, M. (2002) 'The concept of flow' in C. R. Snyder and S. Lopez (eds) *Handbook of Positive Psychology*. Oxford: Oxford University Press.

Philpott, C. and Spruce, G. (2007) *Learning to Teach Music in the Secondary School*. Abingdon: RoutledgeFalmer.

## Further reading and resources

Kellett, M. (2005) 'Inclusion in music in the primary classroom', in M. Nind, J. Rix, K. Sheehy and K. Simmons (eds) *Curriculum and Pedagogy in Inclusive Education*. London: RoutledgeFalmer. This book includes inclusive teaching strategies, case studies about learners and discussion of issues surrounding musical inclusion.

Teachers TV (2008) *KS1/2 Music – Delivering Wider Opportunities*, www.teachers.tv. A video demonstrating the fundamental principles of inclusion through whole class music teaching. It includes examples of teaching strategies, different learning environments and collaboration between music specialists and class teachers.

The QCA website offers guidance and strategies surrounding the planning implementation of an inclusive learning environment for music lessons: http://curriculum.qcda.gov.uk/key-stages-1-and-2/inclusion/inclusioninsubjects/inclusioninmusic/index.aspx.

# Chapter 5

# Musical styles, genres and traditions
## Creating a global musical heritage

*Katherine Zeserson*

## Introduction

### *We're all ears ...*

This chapter is about opening our ears as teachers, and helping open our pupils' ears – finding ways of exploring and celebrating different kinds of music and above all empowering teachers to be confident in supporting pupils to explore and connect with the vast richness of our global musical heritage.

Diverse musical practices offer a wide range of entry points to musical learning (and indeed other kinds of learning) for children across the spectrum of interests and abilities, and are therefore powerfully inclusive classroom tools. Teachers can also draw upon these different ways of making music – and learning musically – and apply them to our teaching in other musical contexts. Through exploring a variety of traditions and styles we investigate the many and varied ways in which people relate to music and how these different relationships influence the way in which they perform, compose/improvise and respond to it – this means that working across a broad range of musics in the classroom creates the best possible foundation for children's lives as musical adults.

Exploring and celebrating a diverse range of musics provides a uniquely direct route to reflecting and affirming the diverse range of cultures present in contemporary society, and the individuals that animate those cultures.

By the end of this chapter we will have considered:

- how classroom music making may be both affected by, and impact on, pupils' cultural identities;
- the relationship between the social context of music and musical learning;
- how different musical traditions can help learners develop a range of skills and understandings;
- how teachers can develop strategies for utilising a wide variety of music traditions in the classroom.

## Music, culture and identity

Music reflects who we are. The astonishing variety of musical genres, traditions and styles that humans have generated across time and place can be read as an exact reflection of our individual and collective cultural diversity – there is no better territory than music in which to locate and explore the richness of what it is to be human. Music offers a metaphor for social organisation and relationships; so a diverse musical classroom becomes a diverse social space, where children can explore different ways of interacting and working together within a tangible, creatively satisfying framework.

In considering the relevance of any particular style, genre or tradition in the classroom context we are likely to focus on three core aspects – repertoire base, technical characteristics and cultural resonance. Given the whole class instrumental and vocal teaching (WCIVT) context, teachers will often make a content choice driven by the second of these – in a mixed attainment environment it will often be important to find materials that can include and accommodate players with a wide range of technical competence. Popular and traditional musics are often chosen for use in WCIVT contexts because they lend themselves easily to this situation. In this chapter I shall concentrate on the relevance of these popular and traditional forms, but will make some reflections that also bear on classical music.

Popular and traditional musics are important – indeed invaluable – in the classroom for cultural, musical and pedagogic reasons. Many children come to school immersed in specific musical traditions, styles or genres either as part of their upbringing or through their own musical interests. They consequently bring to their musical learning in school a particular understanding and perception of music which needs be recognised, valued and built upon if they are to be given full and appropriate access to the music curriculum. Drawing on children's passions and interests in this way helps to make classroom music making more *real* – it is then not an exercise in learning or conforming, but a creative process driven by personal intentions.

In Activity 5.1 we look at ways of engaging pupils in exploring and articulating their own musical passions as well as finding out and sharing their musical heritage. Through doing this you can come to understand pupils better, build a sense of shared musical community in your classroom, engage pupils in finding out about different kinds of music and perhaps reveal unexpected musical resources in your local community.

---

### Activity 5.1 Music mapping

The aim of the project is to produce a musical map of the classroom community – this could be a wall display or a computer-designed document. The musical map should contain information from each pupil about themselves and their family, and also information about the local community. Examples of activities could include the following:

#### PUPILS

- Carry out questionnaire interviews with each member of their household or family – and with each other – finding out whether they have ever played an instrument, what kinds of music they enjoy listening to and what kinds of music they enjoy playing (if they do or have).
- Use the internet to research local musicians to add to the map.
- Work in small research teams to find audio examples of some of the music that people have cited in the interviews and compile audio-visual presentations to share their findings.

#### TEACHERS

- Organise discussions exploring labels and descriptions – what's the difference between Hip Hop and Rave? What's the difference between rock and indie?
- Set up debates in which pupils present their chosen style, genre or tradition and make the case for exploring it in their WCIVT sessions.
- Help pupils plan a series of taster listening lessons or workshops in which different kinds of music from the survey are shared with the whole class by people who really like them – pupils, teachers, parents, other community members, etc.

## Music, pedagogy and joy

Joy lies at the heart of successful music making: joy in our sense of collective purpose; joy in the sonic experience itself; joy in our feeling of personal achievement. There's also joy in music as a community-builder and vehicle for shared celebration. World folk traditions offer us an exciting way into music as a creative community tool – music for dancing, for festival, for ritual, for narrative – and therefore create many opportunities for joy and fun in the classroom; this is of tremendous significance in terms of enabling the classroom music making experience to be *real*.

One of the great strengths of the whole class approach to instrumental and vocal learning is of course that it is rooted in ensemble practice, which is the heartland of music making. Most world folk cultures include a strand of communal form, built to include all members of the community, often within a very structured framework – orchestra, even – that accounts for the youngest members of the community (for that read beginners) alongside the veteran performers. Interestingly, the master–apprentice model of instrumental learning (see Chapter 1) is usually present in these traditional communal forms, the difference being that the dialogue between teacher and learner is conducted within the framework of mixed ensemble practice and through the medium of mixed ensemble repertoire, as well as through mass instrumental repetition. The full inclusion of the beginner alongside the expert can be found in many of the musical traditions becoming popular in our primary classrooms, from Irish folk music to steel band to West African percussion, and the established pedagogic models of those traditions reflect that – whether within the Irish *Comhaltas* structure or within the centuries-old tradition of Ghanaian drumming (Chernoff 1980).

Popular music ranges from material that derives maximum communicative impact out of minimum musical complexity through to intricate and challenging musical repertoire, accommodating a mind-boggling range of instruments, vocal approaches, styles, forms and variants under its umbrella. And there's *plenty* of fun to be had with it ... Some forms of popular music also famously welcome instrumental beginners (indeed punk was built by them), and instrumental learning in pop music has traditionally been predominantly self-directed or peer to peer, although over the last ten years we've seen a tremendous surge in the provision of more conventionally structured one-to-one and small group ensemble pop teaching from Music Services, as well as the development of Musical Futures,[1] which some schools are deploying as a strategy for delivering WCIVT at KS3 (Musical Futures 2010).

In Activity 5.2 we are going to go a little deeper into some of the cultural aspects of music through involving pupils in making decisions about music in a social context as well as making musical decisions.

---

*Activity 5.2 Music for moments*

The goal is to produce a calendar of key events that pupils will then animate with live music, or by choosing and presenting recorded music. This can be done within a class-room community, for the whole year group or for the whole school.

- Decide on the size of your community – the class, year group, key stage, school; if it's beyond your classroom then engage other teachers or staff in working with you.
- Plan a series of discussion and research tasks for pupils investigating how people asso-ciate music with important moments in community life.
- Work with pupils to agree on a series of moments in the chosen time period (one term, one year, etc.) that is to be marked with music and agree what the music will be – and, most importantly, why.
- Establish project teams so that each event is owned by a small group of pupils.
- Make a work-plan with the class to map out what will have to be done throughout the year to prepare for and realise these musical moments.
- Document each event and create a class/school archive.

---

## The nature of the music

It is important to be clear that popular and folk forms are not 'easier' – all music practices encompass a virtuosity in the player's art, and all genres and traditions include more or less populist and specialist areas of interest; more or less complex repertoire; more or less accessible repertoire; and so on. What makes so many popular and folk forms particularly relevant in the primary context is that:

- their musical structures are often built in such a way as to account for players of a wide range of abilities;
- musical interest can be created without necessarily first needing a high level of technical mastery of an instrument;
- repertoire is often modular in form and therefore adaptable to a variety of teaching and learning contexts;
- there is often use of cycling riffs (ostinati) which also helps with inclusion of players at dif-ferent ability levels;
- there is often space for improvisation and variation built into the performative norm, ena-bling creativity and inclusion of everyone's ideas;
- it is often what children and young people are listening to by choice and might aspire to play;
- many core compositional/structural techniques are utilised – call and response, theme and variation, solo and accompaniment, polyphony, ostinato, improvisation – and can be explored both vocally and instrumentally.

*Activity 5.3 Analysis and adaptation (professional development and planning)*

This activity is aimed at helping you clarify your thinking about what styles, genres and traditions you want to utilise in your classroom and why. You'll need to adapt the activity to suit your particular circumstance, the age and stage of your pupils and your own background knowledge and experience. The goal of the task is for you to work with a specific genre or tradition in the context of your WCIVT and evaluate its relevance to the learning goals you've set with your pupils. Work through the points below to help you produce your work plan.

Over the next [term, two terms, year], identify two or three key musical learning outcomes you'll work towards with your pupils – e.g. confidence in a range of time signatures; improving aural acuity; developing improvisation skills; then:

1   identify two or three music genres or traditions that you like and that you'd enjoy knowing more about – e.g. Bulgarian vocal music; Gamelan; Hip Hop;
2   listen to examples of these, bearing in mind the learning outcomes you're wanting to drive at for your students;
3   pick one genre that you think will help you to develop one or more of the identified outcomes – e.g. Bulgarian vocal music to help develop confidence in a range of time signatures and improved aural acuity;
4   using the internet and other sources to identify materials you can use or adapt to your WCIVT context; see if you can find a local musician or teacher with relevant skills to help you deliver your programme;
5   design and deliver your programme of work and evaluate the outcomes – try to map as accurately as you can your pupils' progress related to the repertoire and techniques that the genre exposed them to;
6   interview your pupils and find out how they felt about it and what they'd like to develop next as a result of the project.

## Making the music ...

We *can* animate and explore a range of genres and traditions in our own classrooms even if we are not ourselves experts. This can be achieved through the following.

First, clarify the core learning objective and communicate it to learners – let children know whether the aim is an authentic performance of a traditional tune/song/rhythm; or learning some performance or compositional techniques to apply in making their own new music; or simply using a set of traditional instruments that are associated with a specific genre but using them to play something else, or some combination of the above.

Second, if the aim is to explore a specific tradition, then it is important to get to know the material. If the chosen tradition is one that's not already an area of expertise, then we might invite a performer/performers into school to work alongside us in the classroom to provide expert information and inspiration; but if this is not possible then we will need to research and prepare a set of introductory sessions ourselves. There are a range of good resources now available introducing a variety of popular and traditional genres and traditions. Much world folk music is traditionally learned by ear, which means that conventional Western notated renditions may be approximate or inaccurate, and so when learning from a book rather than a person it is extremely important to make sure one has really got the feel of the music. Listening to recordings or watching DVDs of authentic performances with children and discussing them are all useful strategies – best of all, however, is to listen live by taking children to hear performances.

Third, work with passions and interests from within the community; encourage peer leadership and use children's own knowledge and understanding to guide planning. Apply music to community life – so, for example, establish a mixed-instrument folk ensemble using guitars, tin whistles, percussion and fiddles, perhaps drawn from across several classes or within one class, learn a set of tunes and dances, and then hold a community ceilidh at the end of term with a local ceilidh band anchoring the event (see Activity 5.2).

Fourth, think through the opportunities for inclusion and learning musically that can be facilitated through the chosen genre or tradition. Call and response structure, use of ostinato and drones, cycling patterns, opportunities for improvisation, unfamiliar or lack of notation, different or restricted modes or scale forms and so on will all enable one to adapt the level of difficulty to account for every child in the classroom. Choosing to work with Brazilian samba, for example, offers a range of physical coordination challenges that can be calibrated as required; working with a Gamelan restricts the available pitch range, making improvisation easier to introduce to beginners, and so on (see Activity 5.3).

And a word on fusion – creative fusing and mixing of musics is an inspiring and useful creative process, and indeed musical evolution is built on it. It is just worth remembering that, if ill-thought through, it can lead to a kind of musical brown, with a crude and ultimately unsatisfying blurring of musical specifics; or to a kind of musical colonialism – the superficial collection of exotic sounds and instruments like so many holiday souvenirs. By the same token, over-preciousness about a musical culture can lead to ossification – if we can't get involved and enjoy making that music together without a lengthy initiation or highly specialised training programme then we won't explore it in our classrooms in a spirit of motivated, joyful adventure – and then there's a real danger of that musical culture dying out. Musical languages, just like verbal ones, need to be cross-fertilised with new words, phrases and grammatical constructions in order to refresh and grow. Taking a musical feature or teaching approach from one tradition and applying it to another is a marvellous way of enriching musical learning and creativity.

*Activity 5.4 Cross-referencing*

Take a music style, genre or tradition that you're comfortable working with in the WCIVT context, then:

- identify some core musical elements – e.g. if you chose Scottish folk music then you might identify forms like jigs and reels; or you might identify particular modes; or techniques or ornamentation;
- choose a different style, genre or tradition and look for characteristics that are common but different – e.g. if you chose Scottish folk music then you might take baroque music and look for forms, modes and ornamentation techniques;
- identify some repertoire or pedagogic techniques you can draw from one of these to help develop insights into the other – e.g. if teaching a Scottish jig then look for a Baroque dance tune with a different form to teach alongside it;
- share the different contexts of the different materials with the students and discuss the similarities and differences;
- document thinking and planning, and evaluate outcomes. Repeat with variation as often as you can!

## ... Together

Working in this way makes musical classrooms into places where different disciplines and styles are admired, understood and respected, and where we value making our own new music alongside learning about and inside specific practices and traditions. And, crucially, through music we can explore culture – food, dance, stories, history, geography, politics, social customs, belief systems, values ... and learn to understand and respect other people and other ways of living.

In our increasingly globalised twenty-first century cultural landscape, music is a key means by which we construct and consolidate our cultural identities in the face of – or in response to – change and uncertainty; and so our musical classrooms become critical safe sites for the formation of children's cultural identities. On a personal level, adult rejection or affirmation of a child's musical choices in the classroom environment can make a significant difference to the child's relationship with the adult, and to the child's approach to music making with that adult – or not. All the more reason to ensure that we account for all the children we're working with by presenting a wide range of musical territories to navigate together, and musical discoveries to share. And these children will be tomorrow's musicians – holistic performers, educators and passionate advocates for music's universal human relevance.

## Note

1 The Musical Futures Project is funded by the Paul Hamlyn Foundation: see www.musicalfutures.org.uk. It explores different approaches to music provision at KS3.

## References

Chernoff, J. (1980) *African Rhythm and African Sensibility*. Chicago: Chicago University Press.

## Resources

| | |
|---|---|
| African Drumming Workshop: | www.rainbowdisks.com |
| English Folksong and Dance Society: | http://folkshop.efdss.org |
| Irish traditional music resources: | www.comhaltas.ie |
| Jazz education: | www.neajazzintheschools.org/home.php |
| Musical Futures: | www.musicalfutures.org |
| The UK Gamelan Network: | www.gamelannetwork.co.uk |

# Chapter 6

# Including those with special educational needs

## 'Whole' class instrumental and vocal teaching

*Sally Zimmermann*

## Introduction

We are all different but we expect equal opportunities. There is an irony in that children iden-tified as not coping with, or not able to access, the planned curriculum have an even more complicated structure put around them. Forty years ago this was not the case, and this might also be true 40 years on, when perhaps what makes us different will not be such a mystery. Currently measures designed to lessen inequality revolve around 'personalisation'. We are, however, social creatures and the things we have in common with our fellow human beings are greater than our differences. Sharing music making can illustrate this commonality, this com-munity, intensely and delightfully. The challenge then – particularly in whole class instrumental and vocal teaching (WCIVT) – is to meet individual needs (including those of children with special educational needs) whilst not losing the essence of what makes 'making music together' a rich and meaningful musical experience.

This chapter will focus upon those children whose special educational needs potentially present a barrier to them accessing the music curriculum and musical opportunities which are intended to be available to all children.

By the end of this chapter we will have considered:

- what we mean by special educational needs;
- how special educational needs can be met through drawing on common approaches to music teaching and learning;
- addressing particular special educational needs through specific approaches to music teach-ing and learning.

## Defining special educational needs

Currently children who are identified as having special educational needs are typically labelled as having difficulties with:

- communication and interaction;
- cognition and learning;
- behaviour, emotional and social development;
- sensory and/or physical impairments.

(DfES 2001: 85)

Table 6.1 below briefly outlines the characteristics typically presented by children who have difficulties in these areas.

Table 6.1 Characteristics of some special educational needs

| Communication and interaction | Cognition and learning | Behaviour, emotional and social development | Sensory and/or physical needs |
| --- | --- | --- | --- |
| • Speech and language delay, impairments and disorders<br>• Specific learning difficulties (such as dyslexia and dyspraxia)<br>• Hearing impairment<br>• Autistic spectrum<br>• Moderate, severe or profound learning difficulties<br>• Sensory or physical impairment | • Moderate, severe or profound learning difficulties<br>• Specific learning difficulties (such as dyslexia and dyspraxia)<br>• Physical and sensory impairments<br>• Autistic spectrum | • Withdrawn or isolated<br>• Disruptive and disturbing<br>• Hyperactive and lack of concentration<br>• Immature social skills<br>• Challenging behaviours arising from other complex special needs | • Profound and permanent deafness or visual impairment<br>• Lesser levels of hearing and/or visual loss, which may be only temporary<br>• Physical, neurological or metabolic causes<br>• Emotional stress or physical fatigue |

It is important, however, to remember that individual special educational needs should not be identified and addressed in relation to categorisations but rather in relation to fellow pupils (DfES 2001: 6). From a teaching and learning perspective 'special educational needs' (SEN) is not a fixed phenomenon but rather is an assessment made of a child which is relative to his or her peers. This relativity is often neglected, however, causing teachers to grasp for labels which allow them to map their knowledge or views of, for example, just one person with obsessive-compulsive disorder (OCD) onto all pupils with OCD or, when required to address the needs of an 'autistic' pupil, to go into 'Rain Man' must-have-an-area-of-genius, mode. Knowing, for example, that a child is dyslexic may explain why she did not follow the instructions on the whiteboard but does not help her complete the task you set. What does help is the teacher *knowing* that she is experiencing difficulties in relation to her peers and having sensitive strategies in place that address those difficulties. Labels are relatively unimportant and sometimes unhelpful. Within each category it is important to remember that each pupil still has individual needs and that strategies that might support one pupil may be unhelpful with another pupil with the same 'label'. It is important then that we address pupils' difficulties, *but only where observably necessary*. In other words, we teach the individual not the label. Our concern is about making music and what it is that we need to alter, add or amend for those in our music classes who do not, or cannot, respond to the teaching and learning strategies that work for most of our pupils. However, in making changes we must continue to meet the entitlement of all children to rich and meaningful musical experiences and learning.

As we move on to explore the different ways in which SEN are presented and to find practical suggestions to address day-to-day lesson issues in and beyond whole class instrumental and vocal teaching, we need to hold firmly on to two key principles:

1    That all children are individuals and that we must not lose sight of this in providing for those who have special educational needs.
2    That in providing for children with SEN, we do not compromise their entitlement to a rich and diverse musical education through 'making music together'.

> *Activity 6.1 Observing experienced teachers of children with SEN*
>
> Observe and/or team teach with an experienced music teacher/leader working with children with special educational needs in a whole class instrumental lesson or conventional curriculum music lesson. Discuss the nature of the pupils' needs with them beforehand. Think about the extent to which their teaching reflects the two principles above and what changes you might make to their approaches when teaching children with SEN in your classes.

## Addressing SEN through common approaches to teaching and learning

Although specific strategies may at times be required to address particular manifestations of special educational needs, all that is often needed are minor changes to what teachers typically do in addressing the range of needs within their classes.

### Getting to know the children

This is relatively easy if you are a class teacher, but a visiting teacher will need to talk to the children's class teacher about those children who have SEN and the particular barriers to learning they experience. We have established that we do not define children by SEN labels. Really knowing our pupils goes well beyond simply identifying their category of special needs to knowing their personalities, and importantly their musical likes and dislikes. Music will play an equally important part in the lives of those children who have SEN as in the lives of other children and they are just as likely to bring into the classroom a wealth of musical experiences which teachers need to recognise, value and build upon.

> *Activity 6.2 Talking with pupils with special educational needs*
>
> Find the opportunity to talk with pupils with a range of SEN about their musical interests and what musical activities they participate in and outside of school. Consider how you might use the knowledge that you gain from these conversations in meeting the needs of these children.

### Ensuring the main medium is musical sound

Music, rather than speech, is a medium where pupils, particularly those with communication and interaction needs, may gain fluency, building self-confidence and peer admiration. For some pupils with SEN, music can have personal resonances which can offer a teacher a 'way in'. Getting immersed in whole class music making, where individual contributions may be small but the overall effect is magical, can be part of the awe and wonder of school life and enrich the lives of all children and especially those experiencing emotional and behavioural difficulties.

Music technology and ICT can support teachers in enabling all pupils to engage directly with music making. Musical instruments typically require dexterity and physical control – finger and hand control in particular. Students with physical restrictions and limited control, as with some of those with cerebral palsy, may not be able to develop the fine motor skills required for conventional instruments. Ultrasonic beam systems, notably Midicreator, Optimusic and Soundbeam® (www.midicreator.com; www.optimusic.com; www.soundbeam.co.uk), offer more flexibility as to how to produce sounds, all requiring movement which can be direct, as in a leg or body gesture or a pupil's shifting weight against the back of a chair, or indirect, as in a wheelchair being moved. To play musically in the beam requires rehearsal but can be adjusted to suit individual needs and strengths.

*Case study: A whole class clarinet and saxophone lesson*

Two pupils with cerebral palsy (so limited physical control) in wheelchairs describe their contribution:

It was real music, not that funny 'class music' stuff. There was a pounding Blues backing beat and one team lined up ready to play the melodies and another ready to provide the fill-ins. Then it was our turn. We knew when to move, as we had practised the counting with the whiteboard display, but now we were on our own with sound, and movement. Movement to make the melody, on the clarinet sound, and movement for the saxophone fill-in, as Soundbeam® played our gestures in sound. We can hardly move at all, nor keep our movement under control, so this is how we drive our wheelchairs to play music. And our Blues was poetry in motion, wheelchairs of swirling sound.

*Activity 6.3 Using ICT to support children with special educational needs*

Explore ways in which you might integrate ICT resources (either those identified here or others that you have used) into your lessons with a particular focus on enabling children to engage directly and creatively with music. Consider very carefully the following:

- The particular needs and/or barriers to musical engagement that you are seeking to address.
- The extent to which you believe that this software provides the best means of overcoming these barriers.
- Once you have used the resource, evaluate its effectiveness in meeting the needs of pupils with SEN and consider sharing your experiences of using the resource with other teachers on online conferences/chat rooms.

*Planning carefully for meeting children's special educational needs*

Planning needs to take into account children's learning needs (which we address across this chapter) and the behavioural and organisational challenges that children can present in whole class instrumental lessons. Teachers need to be aware of these issues and plan how they will deal with them in lessons, remembering that most of the strategies that they will use are those that typify good classroom management techniques:

- Have a clear code of conduct, in line with school expectations. Be consistent and, where safe to do so, ignore inappropriate behaviour.
- Have highly structured tasks with clear aims.
- Make best use of the working space and try to avoid bottlenecks when pupils need instruments or move into groups.
- Have a routine for getting keyboards, adaptors, headphones set up by the pupils.
- Establish fun methods of stopping individual, group and whole class work as well as sorting out ways of regulating sound levels.

It is important to remember that music teachers are not working on their own. Each mainstream school has a SEN Coordinator – the SENCO – who is there to support and assist. Some children with SEN may be supported by a dedicated Learning Support Assistant (LSA) and you will need to think carefully about how you will work with them and use their skills and knowledge of the child to best effect. The children themselves can be a source of support as, by the last years of primary education, many pupils are well versed in peer learning and mentoring.

---

*Activity 6.4 Adapting your planning for children with SEN*

Think about a class that you teach in which there are pupils with special educational needs. Note their specific needs (if appropriate in discussion with their class teacher or SENCO) and consider the kinds of changes that you will need to make to your overall teaching plan in order to meet these needs and address the behavioural or organisational challenges which they may present. Also consider how you will work with other teachers and/or learning assistants in the classroom.

---

## Addressing SEN through particular approaches to teaching and learning

Although many aspects of SEN can be addressed through well-focused strategies that teachers draw on to address all individual needs, some children with SEN present particular needs which may require specific solutions in order to allow them to gain access to the music curriculum.

### Children on the autistic spectrum

Pupils on the autistic spectrum may find both non-musical, organisational and the musical elements of your lesson confusing, often for specific, unusual reasons. Working with children on the autistic spectrum presents a range of factors that might impact on their learning. Particular reluctance or rejection in class may be caused by the unusual smell of valve oil or the unfamiliar and disorderly layout of the teaching space. Multi-media presentation, while helpful for others, may be quite bewildering to those with autism. Regular warm ups and other lesson routines may suit those with autistic traits. Teachers may also need to adopt approaches which they would not usually employ. For example, placing the child with autism in a space with a list of instructions or letting him wander around the class without apparently engaging with the musical activity may restrict the sensory input enough for him to learn.

### Case study: A whole class string lesson

David presents aspects of autism. He spends much of his time in class walking around instruments, particularly the string bass at the back of the room. He rarely speaks or joins in: he is just there in class holding his violin doing his own thing, harmlessly but aimlessly. Then one day, whilst working on a composing activity which helps children to develop 'pizzicato' techniques and particularly playing pizzicato with a regular pulse, the class teacher hits on the idea of linking the compositions to the idea of the ticking of a clock. The children listen to the second movement of Haydn's 'Clock' Symphony and also 'Ding, Ding, Ding, Ding' from Ravel's 'L'Enfant et les sortilèges', both of which represent clocks and use pizzicato. As soon as the teacher mentions clocks, David begins to take an interest. He listens intently to the music and sings along with the Ravel. The teacher asks David why he finds this music so exciting and discovers that his grandparents' house, which he loves to visit, is full of clocks, including a large grandfather clock adorned with a picture of an old sailing ship. When at his grandparents, David spends a lot of time just sitting in front of the grandfather clock watching the pendulum swing back and forth. The teacher asks David to go to the string bass and try and do something which is 'clock-like'. David plucks the D and A strings with confidence and maintaining an absolutely steady pulse. This then becomes the foundation of the class's composition.

### Children with visual impairments

Music is an aural phenomenon but, when large groups make music, keeping together is often cemented through visual means. Particularly common in Western music is to have a leader whose main means of control is through gesture not sound. Consequently for every 'performance' there is a preparation and a follow through that is not part of the audible experience. This can provide challenges with children with visual impairments. The example from the whole class brass lesson described below shows how a teacher's actions both address the needs of a pupil with SEN in a sensitive way and then empower him to take a key role in musical decision-making.

*Case study: A whole class brass lesson*

The children are performing their piece without a 'conductor'. The class teacher suggests: 'Let's all get ready to play and be very still. Listen for Joanna who will breathe in a stage whisper, then play the first note together'. Joanna waits and waits. There is quiet for the first time in the rehearsal. She takes an audible breath and the children come in as one. 'What shall we do about the last note?' 'Let's look at someone, let's look at Freddie, and see when he moves his bell round and we'll end with him.' Freddie, like Joanna, enjoys the power, and at the end of the music makes the band hold on for a very long time. Giggles burst out, but the class has stopped together. Freddie doesn't usually have that kind of control over others, often creeping in after the rest have started, and leaving the last note early in case he hangs on too long. Freddie has no sight.

## Children with emotional and behavioural difficulties

Moving around the room without annoying others, not misusing instruments, settling to creative, unstructured group work often without constant adult supervision, having the confidence to finish and present work, understanding the need to rehearse and refine work and putting music and the class before personal needs are all areas that children with SEN can find particularly challenging. Some with emotional and behavioural difficulties, such as those with Attention Deficit Hyperactivity Disorder (ADHD), tend to think of their inappropriate behaviour after it has occurred, whilst the aggression or bullying of those with Conduct Disorders is usually premeditated.

*Case study: Whole class djembe drums*

The circle of djembe drums is prepared and the rest of the class is seated, each with a drum ready to play. Chandeep is outside the classroom with his learning assistant. When he says he is ready, he comes in and sits at his drum, whilst the assistant sits within grasp of the drum handle. Chandeep understands he can play with the others using his hands on the drums, or simply listen. If he feels he cannot do either of those, he is to stand up and the learning assistant will take him to the door. The session flows with very few words from the adult directing. Chandeep joins in after a while, playing at first well in the ensemble and then getting in a muddle, and his playing grows more aggressive and inappropriate. The leader shapes the improvisation to slow down and quieten. Chandeep goes with the flow.

## Children with restricted communication skills

Children who have severe learning difficulties are very roughly at a developmental level of a two- to four-year-old, with the verbal understanding and expressive use of language of that age range. Some children, however, also have considerable language delay and may not speak at all but rather vocalise in a babbling way. This babble can be quite melodious. Encouraging this sound making through allowing silences in music making can lead to children realising 'that's me. I have a voice that can be heard'. For others that silence can be used for making a response on an instrument. Music has the structure to do all the expression without verbal meaning.

---

### Case study: Whole class vocal work

The singing session starts with H.E.L.L.O. from Sing Up, Autumn 2008. The first time through, the backing track CD is used and the class gradually pick up enthusiasm and join in. Then the class is on its own. Michael smiles as the leader clicks the beat to set the pace. Unable to speak, he claps the echo back, louder than the rest of the class can shout it. The leader moves towards him tapping a bodhran drum along with 'This is how we say "hello",' the second phrase. Michael reaches out for the drum (which he cannot see), as he hears it coming closer to him, and copies the phrase on it. The next class activity is a call and response piece. Michael takes the lead, playing the call on the drum, with the class vocalising the response to various vowel sounds given by the tutor.

---

## Conclusion

Remember that children can only benefit from music education if they are actually present. Teachers and leaders need to ensure that all pupils are able to take advantage of the opportunities offered for music learning. Be ready to justify why a child should attend the whole class instrumental lesson rather than the speech and language therapy session. To do this, you will need to be able to articulate the uniqueness of music's offering to children's learning and development, the opportunities (perhaps the only opportunities) that music gives these children to express themselves and the distinctive way of understanding the world offered through musical engagement and experience.

Finally, music itself helps. Some of the children you teach are constantly aware of the label 'SEN' tied round their necks and have peers who expect them to be different. These SEN pupils can play on this label ('You cannot expect me to do that: I have special needs'); others hide behind it and shrink into the background, but much of the time it must be a burden. Ask them, unobtrusively, how they might like to try to do things, what they want to learn and how they want to learn – empower them! Finding ways of including them, and ensuring they learn, challenges our aims and methods. Having a session a week that is presented in music – a different medium from the rest of the curriculum – may be a salvation for these pupils.

## Reference

Department for Education and Skills (DfES) (2001) *Special Educational Needs: Code of Practice.* Nottingham: DfES.

## Resources and support

### Books

Corke, M. (2002) *Approaches to Communication through Music.* London: David Fulton.
A well researched, enthusiastically written introduction describing the value of music to those with very limited communication and then a set of short catchy songs to illustrate this 'intensive interaction' approach.
Shephard, C. and Stormont, B. (2005) *Jabulani! Ideas for Making Music.* Gloucester: Hawthorn Press.
A book which helps anyone to make music. You don't have to be able to read music or follow a song sheet. *Jabulani!* gives you all the tools you need to feel confident about creating music and leading music activities.
Zimmermann, S. A. (1998) *Instrumental Music.* London: RNIB.
A book explaining approaches to instrumental learning for people who are blind or partially sighted.

### Organisations

**Drake Music** (www.drakemusicproject.com) has pioneered music composition and performance for people with physical difficulties through using state-of-the-art music technology.

**Music and the Deaf** (www.matd.org.uk) have pioneered wider opportunities in schools for the deaf as well as writing curriculum-access materials for the national curriculum.

**Music4ASD** (www.music4asd.com) offers resources and training and runs conferences for music education suited to people with autism.

**Royal National Institute of Blind People**, Music Advisory Service (www.rnib.org.uk/music), provide support in all aspects of music making for people with serious sight loss.

**Soundabout** (www.soundabout.org.uk) runs workshops for groups with people with complex needs using resonance boards, beam technology and percussion.

**www.wheelchairdance.co.uk** is self-explanatory!

# Part 3

# Integration
## Setting the scene

*Gary Spruce*

In this section of the book we are going to consider aspects of 'integration': ways in which the range of musical experiences and different aspects of being musical, that children encounter both within and out of school, can be *brought together* in an integrated way so as to make musical learning and development as rich and meaningful as possible. Integration is important because it enables children to understand how different musical encounters relate to each other and how each contributes to their developing relationship with, and knowledge of, music – it can give their musical lives a sense of coherence. For example, within school, children may learn to play an instrument or be having vocal tuition as well as attending class (curriculum) music, and it is important that they are able to make links and meaningful connections between these different musical encounters. They may also be involved in music outside of school, and connections need to be made between these experiences and the music they are involved with in school. Working in an integrated way provides teachers with opportunities to adopt a holistic approach to children's musical development; to observe the full context of a child's musical experiences – the full landscape, if you like – and to understand how their teaching fits into, and contributes to, the totality.

There are, however, challenges which teachers need to meet if real integration is to be achieved, some of which are rooted in the musical traditions within which teachers may have been inducted. Music teachers are products of their social and cultural contexts: the contexts within which they have grown up, have been educated and within which they work. Their experiences within these contexts inevitably play a major role in constructing the values and beliefs (what they consider to be important) that they bring to their relationship with music and their approaches to its teaching. Some of these values and beliefs are underpinned by deep personal reflection and thought. Others, though, are held more subconsciously and are based upon assumptions about music and music teaching which are considered to be so self-evident and universal (because they are so deeply rooted) that they are subjected to less conscious interrogation than those values which are consciously held. Paradoxically it is these values that frequently exert the greatest influence on their teaching of music.

I have argued elsewhere (Spruce 2002) that, despite the presence of popular, non-Western and traditional musics in the curriculum, the processes, structure, roles and values of Western art ('classical') music continue to dominate the way in which many teachers relate to music and teach it. Music from other cultures and traditions are often perceived as simply providing examples of different ways of organising musical materials rather than – as they do – presenting alternative and richly varied models for how music can be engaged with and musical roles defined and delineated.

One of the self-evident assumptions that proceeds from the continuing dominance of classical music, and which impacts on the musical values and beliefs that we bring to music teaching, is that all musical experience can be naturally delineated into the three discrete areas of creating (composing) music, performing music and listening to music, and therefore that this is the way in which music is best taught. This assumption is predicated upon the idea that musical production and reception is a directly linear process underpinned by a hierarchy of roles: the composer (at the apex) produces music which the performer performs to the relatively passive listener, formally seated in a venue specifically designated for the purpose – a concert hall or a building temporarily fulfilling such a purpose. This model is then mapped onto how we teach music and the way in which we organise the curriculum and the examination system: we have 'listening lessons' where children are asked to sit in rows and act like an audience at a classical concert (which to many is an entirely alien, 'unphysical' way of responding to music), graded examinations which focus exclusively on performing, and examination specifications which are organised around these three discrete areas. Composing is the least formalised aspect for a number of reasons, including a continuing belief that only 'special people' can be composers (the Romantic idea of the 'composer as genius'), teachers' lack of confidence in teaching it and the perceived difficulties of its assessment. Unlike, for example, art and creative writing where 'childish' examples are valued and celebrated in their own terms, children's musical compositions are typically measured against adult models. The primary purpose of music education is therefore seen, by many, as the process of selecting an 'elite' who will learn to play an instrument well enough to perform 'great' works whilst those who are less 'talented' are taught to appreciate music as a nascent audience for those who perform.

This division of musical activities has led to the development of discrete areas of teaching 'expertise'. Classroom teachers are seen as those best placed to provide a range of musical experiences that provide a basic entitlement for all children, whilst those that are 'talented' (i.e. have what is seen as a predisposition towards playing an instrument) are taught by a separate group of 'peripatetic' teachers who focus almost exclusively on performance and sometimes just a narrow aspect of this dimension of musical experience: the 'technical management' of the instrument.

This focus on musical 'expertise' has resulted in many teachers in primary schools feeling that they do not have the necessary skills or understanding to teach music and thus it ends up being taught by visiting teachers or music co-ordinators. Teachers are then unable to link teaching and learning in music with the learning that is going on in other subjects. Music is thus disconnected from the school curriculum as a whole (it becomes simply a bolt-on) and children are not enabled to make connections between their musical learning and their other learning that takes place in school.

However, even a cursory exploration of other musical styles and cultures demonstrates that the strict delineation of musical roles and areas is an artificial one. As Francesca Matthews points out in the first chapter of this section, jazz as a style typically rejects the idea that composition comes before performance and that the two are separate activities requiring separate expertise. Compositions emerge from improvised performances and listeners, far from being passive 'receivers' of music, actively comment upon it and, in 'open mike' sessions, become composers and performers. The core musical activities are fully integrated.

Lucy Green (2002) describes how children as young as six form bands working collaboratively across musical boundaries where creating, performing and listening are integrated in the process of deep engagement with the experience of music making. Such musical interactions, and the breaking down of musical roles, can be observed across the panoply of musical cultures which form the musical experiences of the vast majority of human-kind. Equally importantly, these interactions demonstrate that, for the most part, music and musical experience is intrinsically linked to time and place and social and cultural context rather than being separated from it.

The attraction of such musical encounters – particularly for young people – is that they do not distance them from musical experience (push them away by focusing on technical learning or analytical listening) but rather draw them in, such that they become fully immersed in the music. Again, as Matthews points out (Chapter 7), in informally organised bands or through simply listening to/singing along with music or exploring music software packages or websites in their bedrooms, children move freely across musical boundaries, drawing on the skills, experiences and understanding to be gained from all aspects of musical experience in order to gain an increasingly sophisticated and meaningful understanding and knowledge of *their* music. Often this aspect of children's musical lives (frequently to them the most important) is ignored by teachers, examining boards and curriculum designers steeped in a tradition which values only that which is formally learnt and which can be evaluated against those values and processes reflected in Western art music.

Whole class instrumental and vocal music teaching (WCIVT) provide a potentially rich environment for creating the space within which children can become immersed in an integrated musical experience where the artificial barriers between different aspects of their musical lives are removed. WCIVT also provides a context for the collaborative working together of all teachers to share expertise and knowledge and, in doing so, to enable musical learning to be integrated into the school curriculum as a whole. More especially, however, WCIVT provides the means by which children can engage with music in a way in which they instinctively recognise as being musical from the ways in which they experience it outside of school.

In 'Adopting an integrated approach to musical learning in whole class instrumental and vocal lessons', Matthews looks at the core issue of how an integrated approach can support children's development across the full range of musical experiences as performers, composers and critical, reflective listeners. The following chapter, 'An integrated approach to whole class vocal work', sees Vanessa Young consider ways in which vocal development can be integrated into whole class work and particularly how children can be supported in using their voices creatively. Finally Chris Harrison ('An integrated approach to music in the curriculum') explores how music teaching (and particularly whole class instrumental and vocal teaching) can be embedded into the whole school curriculum and the wider life of the school.

## References

Green, L. (2002) *How Popular Musicians Learn*. Aldershot: Ashgate.
Spruce, G. (2002) 'Ways of thinking about music', in G. Spruce (ed.) *Teaching Music in Secondary Schools*. London: RoutledgeFalmer.

# Chapter 7

# Adopting an integrated approach to musical learning in whole class instrumental and vocal lessons

*Francesca Matthews*

## Introduction

This chapter is founded on the belief that music teaching and learning are most effective where teachers adopt an integrated approach. An integrated approach recognises that:

- children learn and experience music both within and beyond the school and these different learning contexts and occasions should inform planning for music learning in the classroom;
- musical learning is at its richest where children are *immersed* in music. Such immersion is best achieved through lessons which involve children in:
  - all those aspects of what it is to be musical – composing, performing, listening and responding – in an integrated way;
  - a diversity of musical practices which reflect a range of musical styles and cultures.

By the end of this chapter we will have considered the following questions, particularly in the context of whole class instrumental and vocal teaching (WCIVT):

- What do we mean by an integrated approach?
- What is integrated musical learning?
- How do we plan for an integrated approach?
- What are the implications of an integrated approach?

## What do we mean by an integrated approach?

Music education has traditionally adopted a 'disintegrated' approach to teaching and learning, with the roles and practices associated with performing, listening and composing being taught separately. The assessment and examination of music learning has typically reflected such an approach and it is not unusual, even today, to hear teachers or children talk of a forthcoming 'listening' or 'performing' lesson. However, even a cursory examination of the musical practices of most musical traditions and cultures reveals that there is often much blurring of lines between the activities of composing, listening and performing. How is it then that music education has adopted this disintegrated approach and adhered to it with such tenacity?

One explanation is the influence that the values and practices of classical music continue to exert on the way in which music is taught and particularly the importance that is attached to 'the score'. Let us consider two musical occasions.

### Occasion 1: The orchestral concert

The concert takes place in a large purpose-built concert hall. The programme consists of a performance of a symphony by Mahler. The orchestra performs from the stage and the audience sits in rows listening in silence but applauding at the end. Enthusiastic reviews of the concert refer to the conductor as having 'really got to the heart of the score' – a significant phrase.

### Occasion 2: The jazz club

The context is a 'Jam' or an Open Mic night. The evening begins with a set from the resident house band, following which the floor is opened up to anyone who wants to take part. Throughout the evening, the line-up continually changes as people perform a number, then sit down again to listen. Those acting as audience interact with those performing, applauding sections they particularly enjoy. The performers react to the audience's responses perhaps by choosing to lengthen a well-received solo section. The performances are personal, often emotionally charged interpretations of basic musical frameworks – a melody and/or chord sequence – which can be interpreted in many ways. Consequently those performing are not just fulfilling the role of performers but are also acting as composers and improvisers. Their realisations of the musical starting points are governed not only by their own personal musical responses but by interactions with the audience. The pianist has a few chord symbols written on a piece of paper but other than that there is no sign of any notation or 'score'.

Let us consider what these two musical occasions tell us about different understandings of musical roles and relationships and how and where 'musical meaning' is created. In the orchestral concert, musical meaning is understood as being created exclusively through the interplay of the musical materials as codified within the score. In order to comprehend the meaning of the music the listeners and performers must be allowed no distractions from a focus on the performance of that score. Consequently the performance takes place in a space which is deliberately cut off from everyday society (the concert hall) and there is standardised dress and layout of instruments; what Durant describes as 'corporate anonymity, so as not to distract from the work itself, or from the conductor's rendering and interpretation' (Durant 1984: 39). Anything that impinges on direct engagement with the sonic materials – talking, coughing, moving around – is actively discouraged. There is clear distinction between the role of performers and audience which is emphasised by their physical separation. The reviews of the concert articulate a commonly held understanding of musical meaning residing within the score, with the primary purpose of the performers being to communicate that meaning to the audience. There is a clear hierarchy constructed here of composer, performer and listener.

Durant describes the orchestral concert (post-Beethoven) as being not an ensemble of musicians but 'a huge instrument or machine which the composer plays by notation; and embellishments by performers are increasingly taken to disturb the overall artistic intention' (op. cit.: 38). Compare this with what occurs in the jazz club. The absence of a score means that there is much less 'playing of the musicians by the composer' and no sense of meaning being fixed within a score – think of the many cover versions of jazz and pop standards.

Consequently the rigid hierarchy of composer–performer–listener is absent, resulting in a blurring of the various musical roles. People become composers, performers and listeners at different points in the evening (even within the context of one number). There is immersion in the totality of musical experience and involvement in creating musical meaning by all those that are present; and this meaning is as much dependent upon the dynamics of the social occasion as the actual notes played. There is little sense of the musical hierarchy as described above as all are involved in creating musical meaning, and musical meaning resides not in the score but in the interaction and intersection – in the blurring, if you like – of those roles. Musical meaning is personally and collectively created – it is a living thing – rather than something which is objectified within a score.

Unfortunately, because of the hold that the values and practices of Western classical music still exert over the way in which music is taught, in the minds of many people – particularly those schooled in the Western classical tradition – the 'score' remains pre-eminent and with it the separating out of the musical relationships that proceed from this way of thinking.

However, this is not the way in which children naturally think of, or engage with, music. They engage with it in an *integrated* way as part of their everyday lives: as 'performers' – *listening* to a song on the radio, *interpreting* it and then *performing* it by singing along; as critical 'listeners' – *watching* and *listening* to performers on popular TV programmes such as the *X Factor* and *appraising* what they see and hear; and as 'composers' and 'improvisers' when sitting down to experiment casually on the piano in a practice room, or on music ICT programs on the computer. These experiences are all naturally integrated, often as the result of an emotional response to music, into the context of their everyday lives. For many children the only time they experience music as a set of discrete activities is in school.

It follows that if children are to see the music learning that goes on in school as relevant then teachers need to bridge the gap between the music lesson and music in everyday life. The music teaching and learning that takes place in the classroom needs to be meaningful to children in the broader context of their musical experience, learning and participation. It needs to reflect and relate to their experiences of music outside of school. These experiences are integrated experiences.

---

*Activity 7.1 Music in your life and the lives of your pupils*

1   Reflect on your own experiences of music in your everyday life. What role(s) does it have? Where and how do you engage with music?

2   Consider your responses to the questions above. What similarities might there be to the role of music in your pupils' lives?

3   Devise a questionnaire to explore pupils' understanding of their own musical experiences both in school and beyond, and how they view these in the contexts of listening, composing and performing. Are these distinctions clear to them? Discuss the questionnaire and responses with a group of children you teach.

4   Compare the pupil feedback to your own responses to points 1 and 2. What are the similarities and differences between your and the children's perceptions of musical engagement? How might you draw on these in your teaching?

## What is integrated musical learning?

We have argued that the richest musical experiences occur when children are immersed in musical learning. To develop both an explicit and implicit understanding of a musical concept, children need to experience it in an integrated way as performers, composers, improvisers and listeners, and to be given the opportunity to demonstrate this understanding through responding to music in a range of ways: vocally (using both the speaking and singing voice), instrumentally, through movement and dance and through talking about it and discussing it. The English National Curriculum Programme of Study (2007: 180) requires that pupils have experiences of 'composing and improvising, performing and listening'. It is easy to have a fragmented approach to this, devising activities that will only address one area of musical experience at a time, and ignoring the equally important requirement that music be taught in an integrated way.

Compartmentalised teaching – that which is separated into discrete areas of musical experience – almost inevitably leads to impoverished musical learning (Mills 2005: 75), whereas an integrated approach can enhance the range of musical skills and understanding. For example, a traditional instrumental lesson which focuses exclusively on the development of technique can miss opportunities to develop other aspects of children's musical learning through composing and listening activities; activities which can actually enhance pupils' performance skills. Moreover, an integrated approach offers many more opportunities to reach the widest range of needs, aspirations and interests when working in whole class settings.

> ### Case study: Township improvisation
>
> A whole class trumpet and clarinet lesson is focusing on performing a South African Township piece, *Pennywhistle*, consisting of several different layers of melodies and ostinati, copy back sections (where children repeat a rhythmic or melodic phrase played or sung to them by a teacher or other pupil) and simple improvisations played with a backing track. The teacher plays a few simple two-note, four-beat copy backs and asks the children to listen carefully and respond through performing their own improvised answering phrase on their instruments. Although the answering phrases the children respond with are relatively simple and short, the pupils demonstrate immersion in the musical style through the syncopated nature of the phrase, typical to the style, unconsciously or consciously imitating the model provided by the teacher.

Within this activity, pupils are clearly focused on one aim – to invent an answering phrase (responding and improvising). But simultaneously the child will be engaged in a listening activity (listening to the teacher's musical question), a performance activity (playing the response) and a composition activity (consciously or unconsciously considering stylistic awareness, melodic/rhythmic shape, emotional response, dynamics). Rather than developing isolated skills they will be learning music through behaving as a musician. It is relatively straightforward to apply the principles of the above to most musical activities, and in fact any practical music activity within a lesson can provide an integrated musical experience.

---

*Activity 7.2 Adopting an integrated approach to performing*

Consider a performance-based activity within your scheme of work.

1   Identify what additional skills and musical understanding might be developed through adopting an integrated approach to its planning and teaching.
2   Once you have taught the lesson evaluate it. What were the outcomes? What evidence of development of additional skills and understanding do the children demonstrate?

---

## How do we plan for an integrated approach?

### Integrating composing, performing and listening

The fundamental aim of planning is to ensure that children develop their musical knowledge, skills and understanding in the context of a rich, vibrant integrated musical experience. David Elliott suggests that real musical learning can only take place within an authentic musical context, 'that, by definition, surrounds the student with musical peers, goals, and standards that serve to guide and support the student's thinking'. He writes that 'music ... ought to be understood in relation to the meanings and values evidenced in actual music making, music listening and musical outcomes in specific cultural context' (1995: 260–267).

As we have demonstrated in the 'jazz club' example at the beginning of this chapter, authentic musical practices are more often than not integrated musical practices. Therefore it follows that the starting point is to plan for musical learning in the context of authentic musical experiences.

For example, a WCIVT lesson has been planned according to the expected technical objectives, i.e.:

• Children will learn to play an F#.
• Children will understand what an ostinato is, and be able to play one.

To truly provide an integrated musical experience, these technical achievements should be *outcomes* that are a result of planning for an authentic musical experience within which the children develop their skills and understanding as composers, performers and listeners. If the focus of the planning is purely on technical progression then it is likely that the lesson will scratch only the surface of all of those things that it is to be musical and thus the child's musical experience will be impoverished.

In the following case study we reframe the development of these technical skills in the context of an authentic musical experience.

*Case study: 'Getting inside' the music*

A whole class violin lesson is focusing on understanding the feel and function of a minor tonality within the context of an African–American work song. The teacher wants the children to be able to identify a minor tonality and describe its character, and then be able to sing a work song and express the feel of a minor tonality through their singing. The teacher starts by playing recordings of music in both minor and major keys and asks the children to describe the differences in the atmosphere of the music. He then goes on to talk about the origins and history of the work song and plays an example of one from a clip on YouTube. The children then learn to sing the song, listening first to the teacher sing it, who models an expressive, mournful sound which, when the children learn the song, they emulate.

To further this learning, the teacher decides to transfer these ideas onto instruments. He sets a simple group composition activity, asking the children to respond to a piece of visual art which depicts a scene linked to the work song genre. Within this activity, the teacher teaches a new note – F#. After sharing their group performances, the teacher then brings the activities together – the children sing the song, emphasising the mournful feel through legato passages and slow tempo, adding in a one-note ostinato on the new note F# to mark the march-like feel of 2/4. He intersperses the group compositions throughout the song, using the tune in a rondo format (the children sing the song, one group plays their composition, back to the song, then the next composition and so on).

Here the learning and musical experiences are extended and enriched. Instead of merely teaching the note F# as an isolated concept, and then adding an easy ostinato to a song the children already know, these broader objectives provide scope for the teacher to be creative in inventing activities that further the children's musical understanding of the nature and feel of the music, and develop it within an authentic stylistic context. These suggested activities focus on musical understanding through which technical knowledge and proficiency are developed as an outcome.

*Activity 7.3 Developing technical skills through authentic musical experiences*

Identify two technical skills that you wish to focus on with one of your classes and develop your own lesson ideas along the lines of the example above, taking care to identify rich, authentic musical experiences as the main focus of the lesson, through which development of these technical skills will be achieved. If you are teaching collaboratively, define the roles of each adult and what they will do in the lesson.

## Bringing together music in and beyond school

The final aspect of integration that we identified at the beginning of this chapter was the integration of the musical experiences and learning that both take place within and beyond school. It is arguable that it is beyond the school that children's most authentically musical experiences take place as these are naturally embedded in a real social context. In this section we are going to explore how teachers can draw upon such experiences in school and build upon these to support children's holistic musical progression.

Earlier in the chapter we discussed how children typically engage with music in a naturally integrated way – where composing, improvising, performing and listening come together via everyday musical activities such as listening to a song on the television or radio and interpreting it in their own way through singing it. For the music they experience within the context of a music lesson to have real meaning, it needs to relate to and be integrated with and emulate these informal out-of-school experiences.

### Case study: Voices unite

Several East London primary schools are working together on a project that aims to promote a culture of music making by creating a massed choir of several hundred children who will come together in a local venue to perform a specially commissioned vocal piece. There is no particular tradition of singing within these schools so, in order to encourage pupil engagement, a survey is undertaken into the pupils' musical interests and pursuits outside of school. The results of the survey show that, amongst the cohort, there is a keen interest in Hip Hop and R&B music, and many of the pupils are church goers and familiar with Gospel-style singing. The piece that is subsequently commissioned is a secular oratorio-style work, based around Gospel-style music, with other contemporary influences such as R&B, Blues, Jazz and Hip Hop. The children are involved in the creative process – the composer works in each of the schools developing sections of the material with the pupils through composing and simple improvisation sessions, and the pupils learn to sing and perform the material through the workshops.

This exemplifies the potential impact of integrating the musical experience into the pupils' out-of-school context – the children have an emotional and intellectual connection with the musical styles, are familiar with the idioms within the styles – the underpinning harmony, role of improvisation, solo sections, singing in parts in a choir, harmonising in thirds and fifths – and are able to accurately interpret and perform the music stylistically, and become immersed in music making. It provides an authentic stylistic and cultural musical experience that is integrated closely with their societal backgrounds and therefore their innate understanding of these musical styles, and is presented in an integrated fashion wherein each workshop session integrates performing, listening, composing and improvising activities which give the children the opportunities to behave as composers, listeners and performers.

## What are the implications of an integrated approach?

What then does integrated musical teaching look like?

First, it mirrors the nature of being a complete musician, where all musical experiences, skills and disciplines are intrinsically integrated, not separated into pockets of individual practice. Translated to the classroom, it is teaching that focuses on the development of an innate understanding of music in a musically authentic and engaging setting which has meaning in the wider context of the pupils' everyday lives and where the development of skills emerge from lessons which focus on musical experiences and outcomes. This may involve a marked change in outlook for many teachers – when lessons and schemes are re-visited, many will discover that currently skills development is the real objective, with the development of true musical understanding a fortuitous chance outcome. If a truly authentic musical experience can only really result from an integrated musical experience, then the focus of whole class instrumental and vocal lessons needs to shift from the traditional development of technical skills to a holistic model that develops all there is within thinking, behaving and acting musically to provide musical teaching and learning in which pupils can be immersed and experience what it is to be a musician.

---

*Activity 7.4 Putting integration into action*

Identify a class you teach in a whole class instrumental and vocal context. Consider the following:

1    What do they need to learn in the next two or three lessons? Identify your musical objectives and technical outcomes.
2    How will you ensure this learning occurs in an integrated way, within authentic musical experiences that resonate with pupils' other musical experiences in and out of school?
3    How will you evaluate the effectiveness of the lessons and how will this evaluation feed into future teaching?

---

## References

Durant, A. (1984) *Conditions of Music*. London: Macmillan.

Elliott, D. (1995) *Music Matters: A New Philosophy of Music Education*. New York: Oxford University Press.

Mills, J. (2005) *Music in the School*. Oxford: Oxford University Press.

Qualifications and Curriculum Authority (2007) *The National Curriculum for England*. London: QCA.

Chapter 8

# An integrated approach to whole class vocal work

*Vanessa Young*

## Introduction

Singing is not only potentially one of the most powerful experiences to participants and audience alike, it is also one of the most natural and universal activities in the world. This chapter will consider the important question of how we get all children to engage with singing and how this needs to become an integrated and embedded part of the life of the school. The term 'singing' will be used in this chapter to include all aspects of vocal work.

By the end of this chapter we will have considered the following issues particularly in the context of whole class instrumental and vocal teaching (WCIVT):

- the value of vocal work in the classroom;
- making vocal engagement a holistic experience which integrates different modes of musical engagement;
- making vocal work accessible to all pupils;
- the importance of a whole school approach.

## The value of vocal work in the classroom

The universality of the voice itself is a means by which we can understand and make sense of music across musical cultures and genres; and engage holistically with music across the parameters of listening, performing and composing. As a universal activity, we need to recognise that it is for all children, and that, whilst singing is an innate capacity, singing competence is learned. Whilst all this might seem self-evident, in recent years this specific aspect of musical engagement seems to have been in the doldrums. The recent report from Ofsted (2009), whilst recognising some very good practice, identified some significant issues with singing. At Key Stage 2, this mostly revolved round the area of quality and lack of feedback and progress. And yet at the same time we have seen a renewed interest (some might say 'obsession') with singing outside the school context with television programmes such as *Britain's Got Talent* and *Pop Idol*; and the democratising power of karaoke, encouraging anyone to sing as a social activity, should not be underestimated. With singing as a cornerstone of the Music Manifesto, supported by both the Sing Up initiative and Wider Opportunities projects, the prospects of getting singing embedded into the life of the school for all pupils have never been so good.

We know that there is a schism between singing in school which is planned, formally structured and 'prescribed' by the teacher, and singing which takes place outside the school in a more spontaneous, organic way, where significantly there is no formal activity or adult supervision involved

(Hargreaves and Marshall 2003). A major factor associated with 'outside' music is the degree of autonomy and control that young people have over their music which they do not have 'inside' school. This seems to be a significant point with implications for our pedagogy as music teachers.

It is interesting here to look at very young children and their relationship with song and vocalisation. Even very young children understand song because, as an ordinary part of life, they have been 'song users' – not just as perceivers, but also as re-producers and even producers (i.e. composers) of song from a very early age (Glover 2000). Very young children show themselves capable of improvising vocally with ease and confidence, often in the context of what are seen as 'playful behaviours'. These song utterances demonstrate the extensive knowledge children have already gained through enculturation (the process by which children adapt to and assimilate the culture in which they live) including: song structures and conventions, cadences, scales, word rhythms and musical movement and gesture. Children know what a song is, how songs 'go', how songs are structured and what people do with songs. This is in striking contrast to instrumental composition which follows a very different pathway with, for instance, pupils needing time to explore the timbral possibilities of instruments before composing (see Glover and Ward 1998). The real shame, as Young (2006) points out, is that, due to lack of expectation and understanding on the part of the teachers, these manifestations of singing competence and creativity go largely unnoticed. 'This rich seam of singing activity … [gets] … squeezed out of educational times and spaces into playgrounds, corridors, school buses, into break times and free time before and after school' (Young 2006: 278).

---

*Activity 8.1 Creating a class songbook*

Ask your class to find and bring a song which means something to them. This might be:

- a traditional song from their own culture;
- a lullaby or nursery rhyme sung at home;
- a song from an out-of-school club or weekend activity.

If you teach children who have English as an additional language, encourage them to bring a song in their own language.

Collect these songs – record the children singing them and write down the words – and compile a 'class songbook'.

Consider what you want your class to learn in the next session and select a song/songs from your class songbook to support the learning.

- Think about how you will use the song. Do you need to be creative with the structure? Might you invent an ostinato to accompany it? Can the song be sung in parts?
- Consider how you can use the pupil who contributed the song. Can this pupil teach the words? Can the pupil teach the melody? Can the pupil lead a section?

---

Encouraging children to bring their 'outside songs' into the classroom not only acknowledges that they exist, but also bridges the gap between 'inside' and 'outside'. This allows the teacher to make links between the familiar and the unfamiliar whilst at the same time allowing for a sense of pupil autonomy and control, and extending the repertoire for all. Children are much less inhibited about solo singing than adults, especially if it is seen as a 'normal' activity, and are often keen to sing on their own or with a few friends – perhaps 'karaoke style', or with an accompaniment provided by the teacher. The child can then be given the status of teacher to help the rest of the class learn the song. Whilst acknowledging and welcoming pupils' 'own' creative work, it is important to ensure that there is teacher input to help to grow and expand the pupils' inner resources so that they are being stretched and stimulated, and not just reiterating what they already know and are familiar with. For example, connections with other songs or parts of songs already known by the class can be made, or invited. The teacher might point out where there are structural features, rhythmic patterns, melodic phrases. It is a short stage from there to invite children to share or make new songs, which may well 'appropriate' and 'play around' with some of these conventions.

## Making vocal engagement a holistic experience which integrates different modes of musical engagement

Singing is not just about the singing of songs, divorced from the rest of musical activity. As well as being a legitimate and valued end in itself, singing and use of the voice should always be seen as integral to any musical learning and understanding.

Allowing children to work creatively with their voices not only provides for self-expression and the exploration of identity but, also, through their musical imaginations, to draw on and apply the inner musical resources they have accrued. There are many ways in which the voice can be used as an instrument through which to experiment with creative music making such as soundscapes, tone clusters, song writing and creating and performing graphic scores.

---

*Activity 8.2 Creating vocal soundscapes*

Soundscapes are useful structures within which to introduce the concept of improvisation and composition to a class, and can work with either a whole class or small groups.

Divide the class into groups of six or seven pupils. Give each group the same title – for example, 'Under the Ocean', 'Outer Space'. Ask them within their groups to experiment with finding vocal sounds which describe the title they have been given. For example, in 'Outer Space', ask one group of children to find sounds which might describe the twinkling of thousands of stars, and another to find sounds which describe a black hole. Work with each of the groups on experimenting with different pitches, timbres, dynamics, etc., exploring how different musical ideas can represent different parts of the 'story'.

Once each group has developed their sounds, the pupils can create their 'soundscape' by directing the different parts to form a class composition. Record the 'performance' and listen back with the class, identifying how successful the soundscape was, and why.

Once you have taught this session, evaluate the benefits to be gained from adopting a vocal approach. Also consider whether the vocal approach created any limitations.

---

It is important not to see creativity and the voice simply in terms of formal composition. There are other ways of developing the creativity of pupils – through improvising and song arrangements, but also through performing (or, perhaps more accurately, 're-creating') and appraising situations where pupils can engage in response, evaluation, analysis, interpretation and realisation.

Creative work is not just about composing/improvising, but includes creative teaching and learning. The voice can be a very effective creative tool in teaching specific musical concepts which may lead to development of specific musical skills/understanding, for example using the voice as a teaching tool within a WCIVT class. An example is given in the case study below.

*Case study: A whole class violin lesson*

A teacher wishes to teach a Year 4 WCIVT violin class to play a new note. The teacher decides to teach the new note through the voice first to help the children to internalise it and understand how it fits within the scale.

- The session starts with vocal warm-ups – activities which focus the class and incorporate consolidation of previous learning. These warm-ups include pupils keeping a pulse on a previously learnt note and copying back short vocal phrases from a piece they know.
- The pupils sing the previously learnt note as a class and learn a new vocal ostinato to add underneath it. The ostinato uses the new note which they are to learn on their violins, approached in a step-wise movement.
- The pupils learn about the new note and understand how it fits into the scale by singing the new ostinato with the notes' names.
- They internalise the new note and its context by singing the new note and the ostinato in two parts as a whole class.

Before the children even move to their instruments, they have a secure understanding of how the new note sounds, aurally how it fits into a scale, and a piece of repertoire to work towards learning on their instruments as their technical skills progress. These creative vocal strategies ensure all children can be engaged and thorough musical learning can take place before they have to deal with the complexities of playing the note on their instrument.

Throughout any vocal work, the importance of vocal health and effective voice production must be considered. Children should always be encouraged to look after their voices and to develop the quality of their singing, and extensive advice can be found in resources such as the 'Voiceworks' and 'Singing Matters' series. Take care that children do not strain their voices. It is important to get a sense of power into the voice through opening up the vocal cavities and use of the diaphragm, rather than 'shouting'. Pupils should always warm up before they sing. This might include:

- aural warm-ups around 'soh' and 'mi' at different pitches (and 'la' depending on age/ experience);
- echo singing/signing;
- making different vocal sounds and sequences involving the tongue, teeth and lips;
- tongue twisters that include meticulous articulation, for example 'A tutor who tooted the flute tried to tutor two tutors to toot. Said the two to the tutor, "Is it harder to toot or to tutor two tooters to toot?"'

## Making vocal work accessible to all pupils

Gender has frequently been identified as a significant issue in relation to singing (e.g. Ofsted 2009). Although boys may enter school with the same singing capability as girls, their performance seems to decline subsequently. Boys become less positive about singing than girls in all age groups even at the primary stage (Welch *et al.* 2009). Ashley (2009) suggests that it is not so much that boys are unwilling, but rather that girls are *too* willing and singing becomes perceived as an activity for girls. Much of the problem is linked not with potential, but with image and identity. When identities are quite fragile in the upper primary years, singing needs to be seen as a perfectly normal thing for boys to do. This does not necessarily mean being taught by a male teacher as is sometimes proposed; getting a 'critical mass' of boys 'on board' providing solidarity in numbers so that they can identify with other boys as singers is much more important. The choice of repertoire is also crucial. Boys are going to find it easier to relate to vocal pieces that are not seen to be too feminine, and introducing them to vocal activities which are perceived as having high status in the masculine world (e.g. a Maori Haka can help here). Listening to the vocal skill and dexterity of someone like Bobby McFerrin can also provide a useful role model. Children's ethnicity and class are other important issues which need to be considered when choosing repertoire.

### Choosing repertoire

The selection of appropriate repertoire is a key consideration for all vocal teaching. The appeal of the song can make all the difference between children engaging or not engaging. We need to evaluate all music against some fairly basic criteria.

### Range

Songs have to be within the physical capabilities of children. For some children who appear not to be able to sing in tune yet, it may be simply the pitch that is the barrier. Most children naturally sing lower than we might expect and within a fairly narrow range and this is evident when observing playground games where children naturally select their own pitch. It may be useful sometimes to let the children find their own pitch, just to get the feel of where they feel most comfortable. The demand of the song also has to be taken into account. For example, melodies that move in steps are generally much easier than those that contain interval leaps. Having said that, if children are attracted enough to the song, what they can cope with in terms of demand can be quite surprising, and introducing more challenge is an essential part of progression.

### Language

Songs need to be evaluated for their accessibility in terms of language. Whilst words and lyrics can be an important part of any vocal piece, it is important not to allow mastery of language to dominate the experience, especially for children who find literacy challenging. This can happen when the words are too demanding to learn or read, or the meaning is too obscure. Having to learn or read endless verses can also be dispiriting for children and distract from the main event – the music. As a general rule of thumb, teaching through the oral tradition seems to work best – developing children's aural skills and allowing the teacher to really focus on rhythmic and melodic content and the development of vocal skills.

*Variety*

We know that commercial music – whether it is pop music or film music (e.g. from Disney films) – has great appeal for children of quite a young age. Whilst this kind of popular repertoire should undoubtedly be seen as having value in its own right, it does raise an important question about how far we should be broadening and extending children's musical understanding by introducing them to that which is unfamiliar. It is tempting to find a 'winning formula' in terms of song repertoire and stick to it, rather than introduce more challenge. To keep lessons fresh and exciting, variety is crucial. Repertoire needs to include vocal material from a range of genres and styles, cultures and periods – chants, raps, choral speaking, folk songs, ballads, call and response songs, rounds and other pieces which involve part singing.

There is a wealth of resources available. The 'Sing Up' website (www.singup.org) is a wonderful starting point with a Song Bank which is described as 'a diverse library of songs to learn and sing, all with audio tracks and accompanying activities'. The 'Voiceworks' and 'Singing Matters' series provide a growing range of repertoire and contain examples of accessible warm-ups and photocopiable songs that range from very simple chants to complex part-songs.

---

### Activity 8.3 Integrating vocal work into WCIVT

Access the 'Sing Up' website (www.singup.org) and look at the section called 'Teachers and Music Leaders'. Then access the Song Bank.

Choose three songs from the Song Bank which complement your WCIVT sessions and which you feel will be engaging and stimulating for your pupils (e.g. if your pupils are currently playing a piece called 'Winter' find a song with a related title; if they are learning a piece with a 5/4 time signature find a song with the same time signature).

Prepare to teach each song in the following ways:

- Download the resources that come with each song (e.g. lyrics, audio tracks, song-sheets, activities, lesson plans).
- Listen to the songs and ensure that you are fully familiar with them and confident in delivering the melody and lyrics.
- Decide how you will teach the lyrics to your pupils. If they need to see the words on a sheet or screen, prepare the necessary resources.
- Listen to the echo tracks which you and your pupils can listen to and copy and decide how you will use the tracks to teach the songs to your pupils.
- Decide whether you will need to play an accompaniment or rehearse with a backing track.

Ensure that the pupils give a performance of each song, either in a formal context like a concert or in a more informal context such as performing to another class.

---

A mediating environment which could integrate a number of the factors that influence access and inclusion could be the virtual one, available through the ever-developing world of music technology, which also has the advantage of being a strongly masculine domain. Conversely, it could also be seen as a way of encouraging girls to engage with technology. A variety of websites allow pupils to showcase their work and receive feedback from peers and comment back which helps develop critical listening. Pupils need to develop the skills and confidence to 'do it for themselves' if they are to gain ownership and autonomy in their own music making (Hargreaves and Marshall 2003).

## The importance of a whole school approach

Whilst some excellent practice can happen in isolated classrooms, it is the whole school approach where all these factors are brought together that will make the real difference. There seems to be no distinction between the kinds of pupils who are more or less receptive to singing experiences; on the contrary, the key determining factor seems to be the schools themselves, or more precisely the leadership within those schools and the culture that is created (Ofsted 2009; Welch *et al.* 2009). This requires a clear vision for the holistic development of the music provision in the school – which sees singing as an integral part of the whole music curriculum but also as part of the life of the school in an all-pervasive way. It is not enough, however, simply to pay attention to 'provision' for singing. Schools need to be aware of strengths and weaknesses and work towards improving practice.

The extrinsic benefits of music have been much promoted of late as a way of justifying music in school. It is indeed the case that evidence for the benefits of engaging in singing is overwhelming and has informed much of the rationale behind the Sing Up campaign. Howard Goodall, National Singing Ambassador, says:

> Research has shown that young people who are lucky enough to learn music and sing from an early age develop better social skills, memory, ability to listen and have more confidence. It can be used to improve motor-skills and language development, as well as cognitive abilities in maths. The skills needed for singing, including coordination and listening, also help develop the brain. Singing also builds a child's self-esteem, promotes team-work irrespective of age, gender, and background, celebrates diversity, facilitates self-expression.
>
> (www.singup.org)

It is tempting to highlight this kind of 'payback' as *the* major rationale for singing in school. This is particularly the case when providing justification for our activities with both senior managers and parents. How much more useful these sound in our logical–rational world where 'value for money' is a core consideration, than the much more nebulous and esoteric aesthetic learning outcomes. We do need to be careful, however, of justifying singing simply in these terms to avoid distorting the curriculum itself and finding that singing becomes merely a 'handmaiden' to other educational goals. The pleasing fact is that we not need to do this. As Finney (2000) points out, by engaging children in true aesthetic education – i.e. singing for its own sake, for its intrinsic worthwhileness – the 'spin-offs' and benefits outlined above will happen anyway. Intrinsically musical goals can achieve additional, extrinsic learning outcomes with no compromise to the original aesthetic purpose.

# References

Ashley, M. (2009) 'How high should boys sing?', *Primary Music Today*, Issue 42, 14(2).

Finney, J. (2000) 'Curriculum stagnation: The case of singing in the English National Curriculum', *Music Education Research*, 2(2): 203–211.

Glover, J. (2000) *Children Composing 4–14*. London: RoutledgeFalmer.

Glover, J. and Ward, S. (1998) *Teaching Music in the Primary School* (2nd edition). London: Continuum.

Hargreaves, D. and Marshall, N. (2003) 'Developing identities in music education', *Music Education Research*, 5(3): 263–274.

Ofsted (2009) *Making More of Music: An Evaluation of Music in Schools 2005/08*. HMI Ref No. 080235. London: Ofsted.

Welch, G. F., Himonides, E., Papageorgi, I., Saunders, J., Rinta, T., Stewart, C., Preti, C., Lani, J., Vraka, M. and Hill, J. (2009) 'The national singing programme for primary schools in England: An initial baseline study', *Music Education Research*, 11(1): 1–22.

Young, S. (2006) 'Seen but not heard: Young children, improvised singing and educational practice', *Contemporary Issues in Early Childhood*, 7(3): 270–280.

# Further reading

Boal-Palheiros, G. M. and Hargreaves, D. J. (2001) 'Listening to music at home and at school', *British Journal of Music Education*, 18(2): 103–118.

Davies, C. (1986) 'Say it 'til a song comes: Reflections on songs invented by children 3–13', *British Journal of Music Education*, 3(3): 279–294.

Jones, P. and Robson, C. (2008) *Teaching Music in Primary Schools*. Exeter: Learning Matters.

# Resources

Sing Up website: www.singup.org.

'Voiceworks' series published by Oxford University Press.

'Singing Matters' series published by Heinemann.

# Chapter 9

# An integrated approach to music in the curriculum

*Chris Harrison*

## Introduction

There is a high level of agreement among writers and researchers (Gregory 1997; Mithen 2005; Malloch and Trevarthen 2009) that music is fundamental to our lives. People throughout history all over the world have made music for a variety of different reasons and purposes, which were recently summarised by Levitin (2008) as to express friendship, joy, comfort, knowledge, religion and love. Given that music is such an integral part of our lives, it is important to reflect this within the curriculum by ensuring that children's music making is not restricted to music lessons alone, but integrated into other areas of the curriculum. Through doing this, children are able to experience music in different contexts and understand how it can be more generally relevant to their lives.

This chapter explores a range of ways in which an integrated approach to music can support children's musical progress as well as their general development, while still maintaining the integrity of music as a subject. The first, and longest, section will look at drawing on a range of stimuli from across the curriculum; the second will look at music within the life of the school; and the third will look at some of the processes involved in making music. The activities outlined will also draw on the other three principles explored in this book. By being *creative* with the musical skills that they are learning, children can explore the possibilities of making music in a wider context. Everyone can, and should, be involved in all these activities ('access and inclusion') – there is nothing to be gained by trying to favour some or exclude others. The activities involve a lot of *collaboration* and understanding of how groups work.

By the end of this chapter you will have considered:

- how to develop a range of different stimuli for music making;
- how to promote the role of music in the life of the school;
- how music making processes can contribute to children's overall development.

## Integrating music with other subjects

Making links between music and other areas/subjects of the curriculum has sometimes been a cause of heated debate. Some see it as helping to broaden the range of musical experiences available to young people, while others think that cross-curricular links dilute the importance of music as a subject in its own right. However, making these links does not inevitably mean that music is relegated to being the servant of the other subjects – the sort of scenario in which children learn songs about historical events or the value of the environment without actually learning to sing any better. As long as the musical goals are clear, cross-curricular links can enhance children's understanding of music and make it more relevant. This general principle is reflected in the Independent Review of the Primary Curriculum (DCSF 2009) which states that subjects will be complemented by worthwhile and challenging cross-curricular studies that provide ample opportunities for children to use and apply their subject knowledge and skills to deepen understanding (ibid.: 10).

### Music and physical development

It is important to remember that making music, whether singing or playing instruments, is very much a physical activity, and that musical and physical development are closely connected. Singing helps children to control their breathing and to extend the range of ways in which they use their voices – not just the pitch range, but also the expressive range. Playing instruments develops muscular control, co-ordination and stamina. For some music groups, such as Japanese Kodo drummers, physical discipline is an essential part of their art. It is also essential to give children plenty of opportunities to respond to music through movement and dance, as these physical responses are an essential part of the process through which they both develop and demonstrate their musical understandings. Emphasising the physical aspects of music making will greatly enhance children's development and progress. For instance, you can help them to feel the rhythm and the pulse of the music they are making by incorporating movements in songs or by keeping the beat with their feet as they play instruments. When listening to music, including music they have made up themselves, rather than asking them to sit in silence, you can, if appropriate, encourage them to move expressively or make up some dance movements.

## Stimuli from across the curriculum

One way of integrating music into the curriculum as a whole is to look at the range of stimuli that can be used as starting points for music making. These can include poems, stories, numbers, patterns, images, shapes and movements. The stimuli can be introduced into whole class instrumental and vocal teaching (WCIVT) as a way of exploring their instruments or voices, or they can provide contexts in which children can apply the skills they have learnt in those sessions.

### Storytelling and narrative

Storytelling and narrative are an obvious place to start. The genre is familiar to children through radio, audio recordings, TV and films which have long used music to enhance the narrative or heighten the dramatic tension, while *The Sorcerer's Apprentice* and *Peter and the Wolf* are well known examples from the field of classical music.

Issue 6 of *Primary Subjects* (CfSA 2009) contains a version of Aesop's fable *The Gentle Art of Persuasion*, in which the north wind and the sun compete to get a traveller to take off his coat. In a music session, children could use their instruments to explore together sounds that might describe the wind blowing more and more violently, or the sun shining gently and gradually getting warmer, or the traveller fighting against the wind and then enjoying the warmth of the sun. In some WCIVT programmes, a class has access to more than one type of instrument. This could enable children to work in separate instrument groups, each taking a character, for example drums for the wind, strings for the sun, keyboards for the traveller. Once children have explored the sounds sufficiently, they can come together to give a performance of the story.

Initially, this can be an illustrated narrative, read by either a teacher or a pupil, with a conductor cueing the instrumentalists at appropriate points to describe the events in the story. Taking this idea further, children could create a piece of music which told the story without words, by following the structure of the story. Another approach would be to divide the story into sections and give groups of children a section each to illustrate (again, without the narrative text). The pieces could then be performed in sequence to tell the whole story.

Similar processes can be used to explore poetry and the imagery we use in poems. Children's own poems can be used as a starting point, enabling them to explore in sounds the images they have already created in words, thereby enhancing their understanding of both verbal and musical mediums.

These activities could take place wholly or partly within a WCIVT session. For instance, the WCIVT session could be used to explore the general idea of creating sounds to express movements, moods and characters. The class teacher could then develop the ideas, overseeing the process whereby groups of children explored and decided upon the range of sounds they wanted to use. They might then use a further WCIVT session to bring it all together into a class performance. The links with language are clear, and children are often able to develop their expressive language by describing the musical sounds they have created. (Much of our language is onomatopoeic – even words like 'whisper', 'murmur', 'clash' and 'trickle' – which shows the importance of the influence of non-verbal sounds on language development.) In Activity 9.1 we suggest ways in which you might develop a project involving music and story to be run collaboratively between the class teacher and visiting instrumental teachers.

---

### Activity 9.1 Music and story

- Select a story to use as a stimulus for music making (the class teacher may be able to offer suggestions) over a period of three to four weeks.
- Identify what skills and understandings in music and other relevant areas the children will develop by the end of the project.
- Discuss with the class teacher how the activities could be shared between WCIVT sessions and other sessions and (if appropriate) what form the final outcome will take.
- Evaluate the effectiveness of the project, particularly in relation to:
  - children's musical understanding and other relevant learning (refer to your original learning objectives above);
  - the organisation of the cross-curricular link;
  - the effectiveness of the collaboration with the class teacher.

---

### Visual stimuli

Visual images are also very effective stimuli for music making and offer clear links to the art curriculum. Similar processes to those described above in relation to storytelling can be used to create music that describes or complements a drawing, painting or photograph. Initially, children can be invited to make sounds that describe what they think is in the picture – for example, activities, characters, colours, patterns, mood or atmosphere. These ideas can be developed through group work and then put together to form a whole piece (perhaps using a conductor to provide some structure and co-ordination).

This kind of activity can support understanding in other subjects as well as art. A portrait of a historical figure, for instance, together with background information about their life, can be the starting point for a descriptive composition. As with the storytelling, these activities can take place within WCIVT sessions or at other times. The important thing is that children can see how the instrumental skills they are learning can be applied in different situations.

### Numerical and mathematical stimuli

It is often said that musical and mathematical skills are related, and this allows us to think about ways in which mathematical concepts and ideas can be interpreted musically. Children can be invited to think about how a number can be interpreted in music. The number three, for instance, can be a three-note melody, a chord such as a triad, a three-beat time signature, or ternary form. The number five could be the starting point for exploring different pentatonic scales in a music session. This can be followed up by the class teacher or in further music sessions, by dividing the class into groups, each with its own pentatonic scale (they can choose or devise their own), to make up their own composition based on that scale. Cyclical patterns are also a practical way of exploring the relationships between numbers, for example by setting a three-beat pattern against a four-beat pattern and seeing how and when they coincide and move apart. Many African rhythms play with the idea of three against two, as well as more complex relationships. These can be fruitfully explored by percussion groups, but also on other instruments.

In Activity 9.2 we ask you to think about how you might develop resources and activities that you can use in conjunction with WCIVT sessions in a school in which you teach.

---

**Activity 9.2 Developing a resource bank**

- Identify a class you are working with and find out from the class teacher any themes or topics they are exploring.
- Build up a collection of resources relating to these themes or topics that you can use as starting points for music making. These could be stories (fictional or real), pictures, photographs, artefacts or mathematical ideas.
- Draw up some plans for how you would use the resources, identifying the learning objectives and some appropriate activities.
- Use some of these resources in WCIVT sessions and evaluate their effectiveness with a view to either modifying the ideas you have had, or identifying further resources.

---

### Integrating music within the life of the school

As well as the content of children's music making, we can take account of the context in which it is made. The music that children make in WCIVT sessions deserves to be heard by more people than just its participants. A large group of children playing music can enhance any of the many events and occasions that take place during the year – religious festivals, parents' evenings, sports days, etc. Sometimes there is a danger of the tail wagging the dog – the demands of an imminent performance can sometimes disrupt the learning trajectory of the class – but if handled carefully, performance opportunities can enhance learning and develop confidence. It is important to remember that 'work in progress' can often be presented as an effective performance. It is also possible for performances to be completely improvised, thereby avoiding the need for long periods of rehearsal. A whole class of children improvising under the direction of a (child) conductor can provide a very effective musical background as children arrive for assembly – but if you do this, you should ensure that they also have some time to carry on playing when everyone is seated quietly. Children can also compose their own music for special occasions – a fanfare for a prizegiving or a piece for Diwali or Chinese New Year based on musical features (in these examples, perhaps a raga or a pentatonic scale) they have worked on in their WCIVT sessions.

In Activity 9.3 we want you to think about how you might develop resources and activities for a special event that is to take place in a school in which you teach.

---

### Activity 9.3 Music for a special occasion

- Decide on an event for which you can provide some music.
- If needed, identify a piece of music that can act as a more specific stimulus for pupils composing and improvising.
- Develop some activities which enable children to explore some relevant musical features of your chosen style or genre – for example, a fanfare is loud and short, a celebratory dance is upbeat and rhythmic.
- Plan a range of activities across a series of WCIVT and other sessions, which result in children composing music for a final performance.
- Evaluate the effectiveness of the project, taking into account the children's responses and their musical learning.

---

### Embedding music in the curriculum

In order to embed music in the whole curriculum, the role of the headteacher is pivotal. He or she needs to be persuaded (as many already are) of the benefits that music can have in supporting all aspects of children's development, and to take the lead in encouraging teachers to make cross-curricular links. With the possibility of schools being allowed increased flexibility in the curriculum planning process offered by a new primary curriculum from 2011, headteachers and their senior management teams can develop exciting and innovative curriculum models with music as an integral element. The role of class teachers is also crucial. They will need to see the possibilities for extending music beyond the identified music sessions. For them to do this it is essential that they are actively involved in music themselves and that a WCIVT programme is not used as a means of giving them PPA time. They may need some support to develop confidence in their own musicality. They will also need to understand how their general skills as teachers can be applied to the teaching of music.

## Music making and children's wider learning: an integrated approach

Music is a social activity, and the processes through which children make music are often as important as the content of the music they make. These processes are important particularly to their wider personal and social development. Music and song are important aspects of social bonding and forming a group identity, so experiences of making music together in specialist music sessions can contribute to this. Creating music in groups requires a range of skills including negotiation, problem-solving, decision-making, evaluating, listening and co-ordination. Music sessions can be designed so that children experience different roles and have opportunities to develop these skills. Activities involving free improvisation in a large group can help children develop imagination and decision-making. Group composition activities can help to develop listening, negotiating and evaluating. Children as conductors can develop leadership skills, while those being conducted learn the importance of following. In mixed instrument classes, they might learn about the different roles that people can take within a group – drums and percussion providing the rhythm, keeping the group together; guitars or keyboards providing the background or the (harmonic) framework; melody instruments taking centre stage, playing the bit we all listen to, but which would be less effective just on its own. If children's attention is drawn to these roles and processes as they occur in a music session, the teacher can refer to them elsewhere in situations that require collaborative working or division of labour, such as creating a large display in the classroom.

## Conclusion

There has seldom been a time when there have been so many government-backed initiatives in music education (see NAME 2009). Taken as a whole, the aims of these projects might be summarised as to make every school a musical school. A truly musical school would be one in which there was music happening every day, in which music was a vehicle for learning across the whole curriculum, in which all adults and all children felt comfortable taking an active part in musical activities, and in which creative music making played a central role. This cannot be achieved if musical input takes place only on specified days of the week, led by a specialist or group of specialists. It will only happen if music becomes embedded throughout the life of the school through the sharing of expertise and responsibility. In this way, children will get more from their music sessions than just the ability to make music in a group: they will see how making music can enrich all areas of their lives and learning.

## References

Council for Subject Associations (CfSA) (2009) *Primary Subjects*. Issue 6: 'Using Stories'. For information about this publication, please contact the CfSA at www.subjectassociation.org.uk. The music section (including the text referred to above) is available on the website of the National Association of Music Educators (NAME) at www.name.org.uk.

Department for Children, Schools and Families (DCSF) (2009) *Independent Review of the Primary Curriculum: Final Report*. Available from http://www.education.gov.uk.

Gregory, A. H. (1997) 'The roles of music in society: The ethnomusicological perspective', in D. J. Hargreaves and A. C. North (eds) *The Social Psychology of Music*. Oxford: Oxford University Press.

Levitin, D. (2008) *The World in Six Songs*. London: Aurum Press.

Malloch, S. and Trevarthen, C. (2009) *Communicative Musicality*. Oxford: Oxford University Press.

Mithen, S. (2005) *The Singing Neanderthals*. London: Weidenfeld & Nicholson.

NAME (2009) *Music Education Update (Bulletin 1/09)*. Available from the National Association of Music Educators (NAME) at www.name.org.uk.

# Part 4

# Creativity
## Setting the scene

*Nick Beach*

Of the four principles that underpin this book, 'creativity' is something of an odd one out. While access and inclusion, integration and collaboration offer either underpinning principles or prerequisites for success in whole class instrumental and vocal teaching, creativity is an attribute teachers and their pupils might demonstrate. So why does creativity get this special treatment? Why not choose communication, skills development, musicianship or any of the other attributes that need to come together to create a musical experience? There is something fundamental about creativity, and the urge to create is perhaps at its strongest in children. Give a child pencil and paper and she will draw pictures, give him an instrument and he will experiment with sound, give them time to play and they will create and act out complex stories. But interestingly very little of this creative urge has been harnessed by historical approaches to instrumental teaching. Indeed the three examples of creative play above are almost diametrically opposed to our image of the traditional instrumental lesson.

The words 'creativity' and 'creative' have tended to have something of the bohemian about them – there is a Romantic notion of creative people being rather different from others and needing special treatment, space to operate or being granted greater latitude. However, in recent years, creativity has come to be regarded as highly valued. Companies frequently list creativity as one of the attributes they value highly in their employees and the so-named creative industries account for over £100 billion of revenue in the UK and employ 1.3 million people.

The growing importance of creativity generally is reflected in the place that creativity is coming to hold at the heart of the UK education system: the final report of the Cambridge Primary Review, *Children, their World, their Education*, reported that the words 'creative' and 'creativity' appeared more frequently in submissions to the review than almost any others (Alexander 2010: 226). The same review goes on to confirm the case for creativity across the curriculum: 'Creativity is understood not only in terms of exposure to artistic and imaginative endeavour but as contributing to the quality and capacity of children's thinking, and to their perseverance and problem-solving abilities' (ibid.: 489).

But for all the prominence of creativity it is still a much-debated concept: what it is, whose creativity we are talking about and how it manifests itself in the work of groups and individuals are all areas which struggle to achieve precise definition. In order to establish a basis for our consideration of creativity in the context of whole class instrumental and vocal teaching we will look here at some definitions that have currency and relevance.

The *All our Futures* report (NACCCE 1999: 29) provides us with a useful starting point with a four-part definition of creativity:

- Thinking or behaving imaginatively.
- This imaginative activity is purposeful – it is directed to achieving an objective.

- These processes must generate something original.
- The outcome must be of value in relation to the objective.

This definition naturally raises more questions. Original to whom? Of value to whom? Lucas offers a rather broader definition: 'Creativity is a state of mind in which all of our intelligences are working together – it involves seeing, thinking and innovating' (Lucas in Craft 2001: 38).

Between these two we can develop an understanding of creativity in music that is not limited to the traditional creative areas of composition and improvisation. Indeed, any area of music making, or any other subject area, can benefit from supporting children to work and think creatively. Further, we can understand creativity as not necessarily producing some*thing* – as in a tangible product. Achieving the creative state of mind has a value of its own.

So whose creativity are we talking about? There is a useful separation outlined in the report *All our Futures* (NACCCE 1999: 89) which makes a distinction between 'teaching for creativity' and 'creative teaching':

- Teaching for creativity aims to support and encourage children's own creativity.
- Creative teaching utilises creative approaches to support children's learning in all areas of their development.

Whilst this distinction is useful, we do need to re-connect these areas for the purposes of music education: it is very hard to imagine children making creative progress unless supported by creative teaching.

A more recent development in our understanding of creativity has been the concept of creative learning, sometimes referred to as occupying the middle ground between teaching for creativity and creative teaching. This approach, where children are encouraged to have a greater creative involvement in their own learning, is discussed further in Chapter 11, 'Creativity and instrumental skills development'.

We might assume that an activity such as music is a fundamentally creative one, but this is not necessarily the case. Arguably the physical skill of playing a musical instrument is no more inherently creative than the skill of typing. Both can be put to creative use and there might be a creative driver behind the desire to develop the skill, but alone they neither require nor produce anything creative. It is vital, then, that music teaching strategies have creativity at their heart, achieving a synthesis of teaching for creativity, creative teaching and creative learning.

But can we teach creativity? The word 'teach' feels an uncomfortable one in this context. John Holt makes a distinction between teachers (as enablers and facilitators) and Teachers (as directors and information givers) (Holt 1977: 26) which might make the word more appropriate. Jeffrey and Woods (2009) talk about 'scaffolding creative learning' which, with its implication that the role of the teacher is to provide support structures within which the child can explore, seems to fit the bill more comfortably.

Further, Jeffrey and Woods (2009: 13) offer the following conditions which need to be met in order for creativity to flourish:

- *Relevance*. Operating within a broad range of accepted social values while being attuned to pupils' identities and cultures.

- *Control of learning processes.* The pupil is self-motivated and not governed by extrinsic factors or purely task-oriented exercises.
- *Ownership of knowledge.* The pupil learns for him or herself – not for the teacher, examiner or society. Creative learning is internalised, and makes a difference to the pupil's self.
- *Innovation.* Something new is created. A change has taken place, a new skill mastered, new insight gained, new understanding realised, new meaningful knowledge acquired.

These conditions will underpin many of the approaches taken in the following chapters. In Chapter 10 ('The creative process') we will propose a model for the creative process and examine a practical example of what this might look like in the classroom. Chapter 11 ('Creativity and instrumental skills development') looks at the concept of creative learning and how this might present us with new ways of understanding the interdependence of skills acquisition and creative development. Chapter 12 ('Realising creative development') examines how creative development can become an integral part of the weekly lesson.

## References

Alexander, R. (2010) *Children, their World, their Education.* London: Routledge.
Craft, A. (2001) *Creativity in Education.* London: Continuum.
Holt, J. (1977) *Instead of Education.* London: Pelican.
Jeffrey, B. and Woods, P. (2009) *Creative Learning in the Primary School.* London: Routledge.
National Advisory Committee on Creative and Cultural Education (NACCCE) (1999) *All our Futures: Creativity, Culture and Education.* London: DfEE.

# Chapter 10

# The creative process

*Madeleine Casson*

## Introduction

Providing an environment where creativity can thrive demands an understanding of the creative process and an acceptance that the outcomes of that process may be hard to predict. In this chapter we will explore creativity as a staged process. This is not to try to pin creativity down to the point where it becomes mechanistic, but rather to recognise that an understanding of the creative journey can make it easier to accommodate and encourage creative thinking in our pupils. The key role of the teacher in supporting creative development is to provide structures which offer a variety of approaches and accept a range of responses and outcomes.

In this chapter we will:

- propose a model for creative development;
- consider what each stage in that process might look like in the whole class instrumental and vocal teaching (WCIVT) classroom;
- consider how this creative model might apply across the range of musical activity.

There is a great deal written about creativity and, whilst opinions are diverse, there are common themes which suggest that it is possible to understand the creative process as a series of stages. This doesn't imply that the stages are uniform or of fixed length – the creative process, and the stages within it, can vary widely. There are times when there is a 'light bulb moment' – the composer frantically writing down the music that is playing in his head or the physicist who has a sudden flash of inspiration – and what we describe here as a stage in the process will be gone in a moment. However, there is still an underlying process at work, and an understanding of this can help us support creativity in the classroom.

## Models of creativity

Philpott (2007) offers a comparison of models of creativity developed by Wallas (1926), Ross (1980) and Abbs (1989). Although differing in some respects, it is striking that all three models propose four stages in the creative process. Table 10.1 sets out this comparison alongside a summary or composite description of each stage.

A musical interpretation of this process in the context of whole class instrumental and vocal teaching (WCIVT) might look like Figure 10.1, which also reflects the fact that the boundaries between the stages are not necessarily clear cut.

*Table 10.1* Comparisons of models of creativity

| *Wallas* | *Ross* | *Abbs* | *Summary* |
|---|---|---|---|
| *Preparation* (preparatory work on a problem that focuses the individual's mind on the problem and explores the problem's dimensions) | *Initiating* (the original impulse): tactile exploration, doodling, playing, chance and accidents | The release of impulse: a stirring of the psyche | Identification of the idea, intention or projected outcome |
| *Incubation* (where the problem is internalised into the unconscious mind and nothing appears externally to be happening) | *Acquainting* (with particular medium): conversant with sound, practice, further exploration | Working in a medium | Playing with the idea – thinking around it – considering possibilities |
| *Intimation* (the creative person gets a 'feeling' that a solution is on its way), leading to *illumination* or insight (where the creative idea bursts forth from its preconcious processing into conscious awareness) | *Controlling* (mastery of techniques/skills to manipulate parameters of music): constraints and limitations | Critical judgement moves towards the realisation of a final form | Refining ideas and developing the necessary skills |
| *Verification* (where the idea is consciously verified, elaborated and then applied) | *Structuring* (gathering into a satisfying whole) | Presentation and performance/responses and evaluation by the community | Structuring, presenting and evaluating the result |

**Identification of the idea**

What is the musical challenge?
How will we approach the solution?
What do we want to achieve?

**Playing with the idea**

Musical pondering
Exploring sound
Playing with musical ideas
Musical doodling

**Refining ideas and developing skills**

Ideas become reality
Making improvements
Musical choices
Developing required skills

**Structuring, presenting and evaluating**

Performing
Evaluating
Celebrating

*Figure 10.1* A musical model of the creative process

In this chapter we will explore each stage of this model and consider how it might look in practice. In order to do so we will take as our case study a single WCIVT composition project and explore it through each of the four stages. It is important to recognise that, although we use a composition example for the case study here, every aspect of musical learning and experience – performing, composing, listening and appraising – has the potential to be a creative activity and can be mapped against the same staged process.

## Stage one: identification of the idea, intention or projected outcome

One way of understanding the starting point for creativity is to think of 'the problem' that the creative process is trying to 'solve'. The problem can take a wide variety of guises: 'How am I going to communicate this mood/feeling?', 'How are we going to compose a piece for this event?', etc. This implies some important questions:

- What is the problem that we are trying to solve?
- Whose problem is it?
- Whose solutions are we interested in?
- Who will have ownership of the result?

Often in classroom projects the initial impetus will come from the teacher. Whilst we should have starting points and activities planned, these should be designed in such a way that they encourage the child to take ownership of the problem, to frame it in their own way and to develop an understanding of why the result might be important.

Taking the time to explore the nature of the activity or challenge in this early stage can help to ensure that children have a clear creative role and ownership. This may mean that things take some unexpected turns but it can be these which produce the most interesting results.

So how might this first phase of the creative process look in the classroom? In our case study the class have been learning about the planets and space as part of their geography and literacy topic work. The class teacher and visiting instrumental teacher are keen to make links between this learning and their WCIVT programme. At the end of the term the class will lead an assembly for the rest of the school to showcase their work.

---

### Case study: Moon landing part one

In their weekly lesson the class teacher explains that they will be working on a piece of music which will link to their 'Planets and Outer Space' topic. There is a discussion of the possible options and the children share some enthusiastic ideas:

- Should they create a totally new piece or take a song/piece that they already know and develop this?
- Will the music take the form of musical 'accompaniment' to the display of their geography and literacy work or do they want to provide a specific 'performance' piece which also showcases their musical and instrumental learning?

The children discuss what sort of resources might help them in the early stages. They bring into the class some of the pictures they have been using and talk about a video documentary they have watched. The teacher offers to bring in some recordings of music inspired by space.

There is further discussion and the class decide that they want to create their own performance piece which is a musical backing track to the moon landing video. Watching the video they put together a list of words and ideas that describe the sort of atmosphere they want the piece to evoke.

*Activity 10.1 Applying the creative process to musical problem-solving*

- Think of three musical 'problems' to which the creative process might apply, for example creating the right mood for a piece, understanding a new musical concept, composing a piece for an occasion.
- Note down some ways of helping your class to take ownership of each 'problem', referring to the questions at the start of stage one.

## Stage two: playing with the idea – thinking around it – considering possibilities

Perhaps this is the phase in the creative process which is most common across all creative activity, seen in the artist's sketchpad, creative team discussions, a composer's playing with musical ideas or a designer's doodling. Creators need to find space for this sort of exploration – for some it might be long walks in the country or the assurance of uninterrupted thinking or discussion time. This provides a gestation period where ideas are followed, developed, discarded, reviewed, etc. It is seldom a straight-line process – creators, working individually or together, will often go round in circles, meeting frequent dead ends and returning to try other avenues. The image of the writer with an ever-filling wastepaper basket next to their desk is perhaps one of the most powerful visual representations of this phase.

Supporting this developmental phase in WCIVT sessions presents challenges. Initially the children will need help and guidance in exploring ideas and they will need to be assured that every contribution is valued and worthwhile – all within a timely framework which might not allow for long country walks!

Although the distinction between composition and improvisation is often blurred, it is at this stage that improvisation will often be the main focus. What might start off as a simple call and response activity can quickly move on to giving the children space to produce musical fragments and ideas. These can form the building blocks in a musical version of the 'artist's sketchbook' activity where a bank of ideas are stored which can be developed at a later date. IT and recording technology present the ideal way for pupils to begin to build a repertoire of ideas which they can see building over time, perhaps through an 'audio sketchbook' where individuals or groups can record work.

This concept of 'playing about with ideas' is not just relevant to composition but is important for all types of creative musical activity. A student learning a new piece might 'play about' with different interpretations, perhaps seeing what would happen if it was played in a range of different ways, asking what impact this would have on the mood of the performance, etc.

*Case study: Moon landing part two*

The following week, as part of their string WCIVT project, the class watch the moon landing video again. The children recount different episodes of the story: the countdown, the
moon landing, the opening of the shuttle door and the first steps on the moon – these are
listed on the board.

As a class they revisit the word list they made last week and, using instruments and
voices, experiment with how these can be represented in sound. The children work in
pairs and, at regular intervals, innovative or interesting examples are shared with everyone and then discussed. Each of these is then linked to a particular episode of the video.
Altogether they create graphic representations of the shapes of the sounds which are also
recorded using an MP3 device.

---

*Activity 10.2 Playing with ideas*

- Select one of the pieces that your class is learning and have a discussion with them
  about how it is possible to play the piece in different ways to create different moods.
- Divide the children up into groups and ask them to use the first few notes to create
  three very short mood fragments.
- Allow each group to perform some of their work and have a discussion about how the
  mood is created in each case.

---

## Stage three: refining ideas and developing the necessary skills

The key features of this stage are the application of critical judgement in defining, and refining, the ideas, possibly requiring the development of the skills required to produce a successful
outcome.

Through the process of playing about with ideas in the previous phase, a hierarchy will begin
to emerge, and it is this that marks the third phase in this process. Some ideas will fire the children's imagination and enthusiasm, others will be discarded. Ideas will be refined and developed
in this stage so that they have a clear application. In the context of performance this might mean
that several ways of playing something have been discarded and a preferred solution is emerging.
Pupils working on composition will be going through the same process – using critical listening
and appraising to make decisions about how they can improve or develop a chosen idea.

Controlling and refining ideas may involve improving existing skills or developing new ones
to facilitate the desired outcome, always ensuring that the focus of the skill is on achieving the
musical effect as opposed to technical mastery for its own sake.

*Case study: Moon landing part three*

Having explored and experimented with a variety of sounds, the class are going to choose and refine their 'working palette' of musical ideas which will become the building blocks of their composition. Their focus for today's lesson is to identify the sounds that would be most suitable for the opening of the shuttle door after it has landed on the moon.

The children revisit the graphic representations and audio clips from the previous weeks' lessons and choose the idea which they think would be most appropriate – a rasping sound. The sound was produced using rapid bowing on the G string close to the bridge, and the pair who created it model the sound and then explain how they play it before everyone else joins in. Another pupil suggests the sound could start quietly and get louder so they try to do this. The teacher explains that this is called a crescendo.

A second child suggests there should be a sudden silence after the crescendo to depict the silence heard after the shuttle door has opened. They all agree that this would work well. The class agree that the child who made this suggestion should conduct it so that they stop together.

---

*Activity 10.3 Experimenting with musical ideas*

Following on from Activity 10.2:

- Ask the class to discuss which of the mood fragments created in their groups were particularly successful and help them select two or three which they will apply to the piece they are learning.
- Again working in groups, ask them to work at these two or three versions to try and get them really good. Make it clear that if they need help they should ask and one of the teachers will come to their group.
- Ask each group to select one of their versions to perform to the class and have a class discussion about what skills were needed to make an effective performance.

## Stage four: structuring, presenting and evaluating the result

By the time the fourth stage of the creative process is reached, the end point becomes the focus of activity. Commonly for composition and performance-based work this will involve a public sharing of some kind where the end result of the creative process can be shown to an audience. Preparation for this event will give children new enthusiasm and energy.

In this refining and rehearsing stage it is important to consider the importance of communicating what has been produced to the audience. Communication is an integral feature of any performance. It is worth taking time to prepare for performance so that children are able to focus on communicating the meaning of their music and preserving the integrity of their original ideas.

Finally, evaluation and reflection will complete the creative process. Here we can invite pupils to consider what we set out to achieve back in stage one. This provides the opportunity for children to develop their own judgements through considering the extent to which they have achieved their objectives. Evaluation itself can be treated as a creative activity, with children encouraged to take ownership of the problem and to discuss possible solutions. As well as exploring and evaluating any outcomes it is vital that the creative process itself is evaluated. To what extent did children act as creators? To what extent did the teachers act as co-creators? How much did children take the lead? Considering and acting on the answers to questions such as these will support the development of both teachers and their pupils.

---

*Case study: Moon landing part four*

As a class the children decide they would like to have the moon landing video showing in the performance so this will mean the episodes are matched to the footage – providing the structure. They experiment with all the class playing all the episodes and then with each episode being taken by a small group. After discussion they agree that it makes the transition simpler if they use small groups, but that the first and last sections will be with everyone playing.

For the first full run-through, the teacher directs proceedings, cueing the entry of each of the groups. The teacher then puts the 'moods' word list up on the board. There is a discussion about whether each section is creating an appropriate mood. Each of the groups goes off and works on their own section for a while – each has a group leader who takes responsibility. The next full run-through is much more successful and less dependent on the teacher's direction.

The music is recorded and added as a sound track to the video. The teacher plays the video without any backing track and then plays it again with the sound track. The class agree that the version with music creates a much more powerful mood and they are pleased with the result.

The final result is both a live performance to parents and a recording which is uploaded to the school's website.

---

*Activity 10.4 The creative process in practice*

- Think of an activity or project you have recently concluded with your class – it might be a performance, a composition, etc.
- Map the activity onto the four-stage creative process outlined in this chapter, thinking about how much time each stage took and how it was supported.

Consider what changes you might make when supporting this activity on future occasions.

## Conclusion

According to Bruner, 'In as far as possible, a method of instruction should have the objective of *leading the child to discover for himself*'. The virtue of such an approach is that the 'child will make what he learns his own' (1965: 123).

This chapter has explored the creative process as expressed in four stages. We have acknowledged that there is a degree of artificiality about any such division but it does present a useful way of analysing and supporting the phases that children will go through on their creative journey. Although plans for creative work benefit from acknowledging these phases, they should not be treated as a blueprint and there is no expectation that one stage will be completed before the next is started. Looking at a composition project in these terms has allowed us to unpack these stages, but we have acknowledged how they might be reflected in all whole class instrumental and vocal work.

Perhaps with all approaches to creativity the key to success is ownership. The pupil who is instructed and coached to the point where they are able to produce what the teacher wants them to produce has arguably had an arid musical experience. The pupil who has been supported on their own musical voyage of discovery will own the result and will be the richer for it.

## References

Abbs, P. (1989) *A is for Aesthetic: Essays on Creative and Aesthetic Education*. London: Falmer Press.
Bruner, J. (1965) *On Knowing Essays for the Left Hand*. New York: Atheneum.
Philpott, C. (2007) *Learning to Teach Music in the Secondary School*. London: Routledge.
Ross, M. (1980) *The Arts and Personal Growth*. London: Pergamon.
Wallas, G. (1926) *The Art of Thought*. London: Watts.

## Chapter 11

# Creativity and instrumental skills development

*Nick Beach*

## Introduction

Playing a musical instrument involves some of the most demanding combinations of physical, aural and visual skills in human achievement. The reaction of instrumental specialists to this has often been to rely on drills and routines, separate from the business of making music or acting creatively, as the perceived direct route to technical competence. This has frequently been seen as a 'simple' process of the teacher passing their skills to the child – 'you just tell 'em' as a teacher once summarised the process to this writer! It is ironic that making music, an activity which is so rooted in creativity, can become so uncreative in its teaching and learning.

The relationship between creativity and skills development is a complex one. The main point of learning a musical instrument is to make music – to create and communicate musical meaning. In order to do that, children need a set of skills, including technical instrumental skills. However, to treat these separately from the business of making music not only reduces them to arid activities but also takes away the main driver for developing the skill in the first place. The child who is learning a new skill in order to be able to communicate something they have created effectively will do so much more quickly than the child who is repeating routines without a genuine understanding of their musical purpose.

> For me, learning to play the piano was as natural as learning to walk. My father had an obsession about wanting things to be natural. I was brought up on the fundamental principle that there is no division between musical and technical problems.
>
> (Daniel Barenboim quoted in Booth 1999: 88)

In this chapter we argue that through creative learning, which supports children to act creatively, we can provide opportunities for developing musical skills and understanding at a much deeper level.

By the end of the chapter we will have considered how, through embedding skills development within creative learning, we can:

- offer teachers and children in whole class instrumental lessons an alternative to the traditional 'drilling' approach to instrumental skills development;
- give children greater ownership over their musical learning;
- encourage peer creative learning within whole class instrumental and vocal lessons.

## Learning to do – or doing

Most people would say that what I am doing is 'learning to play the cello' ... These words carry into our minds the strange idea that there exist two very different processes: 1) learning to play the cello; and 2) playing the cello ... Of course, this is nonsense. There are not two processes, but one. We learn to do something by doing it.

(Holt 1977: 17)

### Case study: A whole class brass and woodwind lesson

A class of clarinets and trumpets perform *C Jam Blues* – a piece in the big band style which only uses two notes. When they play they *are* a big band – they move, swing, look and feel like a big band. Despite their limited resources they are experiencing what it is to be a musician. Their technical development is a part of this of course, but only one part that supports the whole and a means to an end rather than an end in itself.

If we agree with Holt that, in music, learning to do is the same thing as doing, then it is absolutely vital that everything we 'do' is about music. In a 2006 radio interview, Daniel Barenboim expressed the view (paraphrased) that 'the fingers should never be given permission to do anything unmusical' and this supports Swanwick's belief that 'care for the music must be at the heart of what we do' (Swanwick 1999). The implication of both of these views is that everything we encourage children to do must be about music so that they begin to understand what it is like to be a musician from the very first lesson: they make decisions based on musical judgement, they listen and they explore possibilities.

In the lesson featured in the following case study, which is taught by a visiting string specialist and the classroom teacher, we look at two possible directions the lesson might take.

### Case study: Learning a new note

A whole class group of violinists who up to now have only played with open strings are about to take their first steps playing fingered notes. The teacher demonstrates the technique and the whole group plays open E and F# alternately in a series of copycat rhythms, against a Samba percussion backing, led by the teacher. Some children do this very much more successfully than others ...

#### APPROACH A

They then split into groups of three and are given the task of producing a short Samba-style pattern which uses these two notes. As they work the teachers visit each group offering support and answering questions. The children are invited to perform their pattern to the rest of the class which they do with fluency, in tune and with a relaxed bow hold. The lesson concludes with discussion about the process and what the problems were.

#### APPROACH B

The instrumental teacher continues the copycat exercise while the classroom teacher helps some children who are finding it difficult. A piece using the two notes is put on the whiteboard – the teacher shows the class which note is which, demonstrates the piece and begins to teach it to them. Through a combination of modelling and following notation most of the children learn the piece reasonably effectively but lack the fluency and ease of those children in approach A.

In this case study we might describe the activity in approach A as improvisation, composition or some combination of the two. However, what is important here is that the development of the new skill is embedded within a creative and musical activity. The technical goal is achieved through creative means – through engaging the children in the learning process and giving them some control. Although both have their merits, approach A offers a much richer musical experience. In approach A, children are engaged in what Jeffrey and Woods (2009: 71) describe as 'operation, risk taking, experimentation and problem solving'. There is a clear reason for developing the skill – it will allow them to communicate their own musical ideas more effectively. There are skills being developed in approach B as well of course, but the reasons for their development and the musical use to which they will eventually be put is less clear.

It is also noticeable that because musical and creative aspects are emphasised rather than technical and note-reading ones, the children are able to focus more on the music. The complexities involved in the performance of music from notation are immense and frequently lead the player to give 'the dots' the primary focus. Once these are removed the player is free to focus on other areas and is much more likely to be able to listen critically to the end result and to be aware of the physicality of playing the instrument.

---

*Activity 11.1 Thinking about creativity and technical development*

- Think of a technical skill that you have recently taught your class and the way you taught it.
- Consider whether your teaching mostly reflects approach A or approach B.
- What changes might you make if you were teaching this skill again in order to embed the development of the skill in creative activity?

---

## Creative learning

Craft (2005: 55) states: 'facilitating the evolution, expression and application of children's own ideas forms the heart of "creative learning", which … engages children powerfully in knowledge production'. Creative learning is emergent as a concept and as yet does not have a precise definition, but might be described as having the following features:

- The teacher is not an instructor but a co-creator, supporting children as they develop their own learning.
- Teachers are constantly looking for ways of engaging children's imagination and invention.
- Children are supported in taking risks – to ask 'what if?' and then go ahead and try it.
- Children are encouraged to evaluate and assess their own and each other's work.

Creative learning has the potential to bring about a deeper and more fundamental change in the child but it requires a degree of risk taking and courage from the teacher in order to support it. Arguably it is at the opposite end of the spectrum to the way in which instrumental skills have traditionally been developed but is entirely consistent with Barenboim's and Swanwick's statements above. What it suggests is that we might develop environments within which children's own imaginations are engaged with all aspects of making music, including the development of skills.

---

### Case study: A whole class woodwind lesson

The classroom and instrumental teachers have planned a project based on 1920s jazz. In the instrumental lessons the children have been working on a 1920s-style jazz piece and improvising sections of the music in typical trad-jazz fashion. In their art lessons the children have been looking at Picasso's *Three Musicians*,[1] discussing how it was constructed and working at collage representations of musicians at work.

In the instrumental lesson the teacher then poses the question, 'What might you do if you were to create a musical version of the picture?' and asks them to discuss this in small groups. After a few minutes a child in one group suddenly has a 'eureka moment'. He makes the link between the jigsaw nature of the painting and using this as the basis for a composition. This creative linking acts as a catalyst for the rest of the group. Another member of the group suggests that they take bits of tunes and play them at the same time. They feed back these ideas to the rest of the class and this ignites the imagination and inventiveness of the children. Ideas come flying in: one pupil suggests taking the jazz tune that they have been working on for the last three weeks and using fragments of this, combining them in different ways.

Enthused by their own ideas, the children go back into groups to work on their compositions, returning after 15 minutes to perform and record them.

They then discuss how effective they have been in representing the ideas in, and the structure of, the painting.[2]

---

Making links is an important feature of creative learning, not just because it supports a constructivist view of learning where children build new knowledge on existing foundations, but because it harnesses the imagination in deepening learning. In this case study the pupils make creative links both within the musical domain and beyond it. Being creative is about making such links and then using them in new ways which are likely to bring about a more fundamental understanding of clarinet technique than drilling and repetition alone.

---

### Activity 11.2 Creating a context for creative learning

- Analyse the above case study in terms of the extent to which it meets the characteristics of 'creative learning' as set out above. How could the activities be developed in which teachers 'act as co-creators' and 'look for ways to engage children's imaginations'?
- Discuss with colleagues (other musicians and other creative arts teachers) how you might devise a similar project. As you plan, keep referring to the characteristics of creative learning, ensuring that what you do provides opportunities for these.
- Evaluate the effectiveness of the lesson against these characteristics.

## Peer creative learning within whole class instrumental lessons

As was seen in the previous case study, working in small groups within the context of whole class lessons can provide an ideal environment for creative learning: children become co-creators with each other, feeding off each other's imagination, supporting each other to experiment and take risks and evaluating and reflecting on the result. It also offers benefits in terms of skills development:

- Children are able to work at their own level.
- Children with a higher level of skill can be used as a resource.
- Peer examples offer achievable goals.

Peer learning has been advocated extensively through the *Musical Futures* approach in the UK. This is based on 'a more democratic way of learning – utilising the skills within the group through peer learning, teachers shedding the mantle of "expert", students and teachers co-constructing content and objectives for sessions' (D'Amore 2009: 45), and in such a way reflects one of the characteristics of creative learning as being that where the teacher is not seen as an instructor but a co-creator.

Thought of in this way, the small group can become an environment where skills are shared as the solutions to particular problems are sought. The problems are those established as such by the children, who seek out solutions, encounter stumbling blocks, access support and achieve results.

### Case study: Peer learning

A whole class group of trumpets is learning a piece called *Toreador's March* which introduces them to playing a new note. The class have previously developed a word list that describes the mood that they are trying to evoke and in today's lesson they are looking at the opening fanfare section which is based on three notes – two notes they have learnt plus the additional 'new note'. The teacher splits the class into groups of five, ensuring that there is a good mix of attainments in each group. The groups are given the task of experimenting with different ways of playing this section and relating these to different words on the list. They then choose one word and one way of playing the section and demonstrate this to the rest of the class. The class decide which word they think they are trying to represent and to use musical (though not necessarily technical) language in describing these. The two teachers go around the groups to offer technical support as necessary – in some of the groups there is a child who has higher level skills and these require a little less time from the teachers.

This case study exemplifies an approach to skills development which is the antithesis to technical drilling. Here the process starts with the identification of a musical problem within which the development of a particular technical issue is embedded. Although the teacher has set the parameters, the children themselves have defined the problem: how to play these notes so as to represent the mood they wish to establish. The children then work together on providing a solution to that problem, drawing on external expertise (the teachers) as appropriate. The success of their approach is provided not by the approbation of the teacher but by their success in solving the problem, i.e. communicating their chosen mood to the remainder of the class.

*Activity 11.3 Embedding creativity in teaching technical development*

- Identify a technical skill that you want the children to develop.
- Embed the learning that they will need to do in order to develop this skill within a musically creative context.
- Decide how you are going to create opportunities for children to support each other in identifying and achieving their musical goals.

Following the lesson:

- Evaluate how well it worked – did the children find it easy to meet their own criteria?
- List the creative ways they found to support each other's learning.

## Conclusion

Our aim as music teachers is to help young people experience what it is to be a musician: someone who makes musical decisions and expresses themselves in a unique and rewarding way. The technical challenge of learning an instrument is considerable, however, and for many that leads to a *Gradus ad Parnassum* approach where technical development is seen as sequential, with each skill being drilled in before the next can be tackled. The effect of this on the learner is similar to a series of hurdles, each higher than the next, with only those that can jump the highest gaining the rewards available at Parnassus.

We know that the techniques and skills involved in making music are complex and there is a right way, or at least a limited number of right ways, to do things. Creative learning does not imply that children should be allowed to play how they like and that we should abandon centuries of learning about what constitutes effective technique. Children need to be able to control the instrument effectively in order to use it to communicate musical ideas and we know a lot about the physical requirements that will facilitate that control.

What creative learning offers us, however, is an alternative route where skills development is driven by creative impulse through 'offering pupils opportunities to shape new knowledge' (Craft 2005). But to take this alternative path, teachers will need to take risks and to accept that some of the outcomes may not be those they expected. If we are to hand some control of learning over to children, we are also handing over some control over the outcomes from that learning. Our role might be seen less as teachers and more as facilitators of learning, or constructors of the scaffolding that supports learning. But whatever uncertainty there may be about precise outcomes, one thing we can be certain of is that children who are actively engaged in creative learning in music are gaining a deeper insight into what it is to be a musician.

## Notes

1  See http://en.wikipedia.org/wiki/Three_Musicians.
2  Adapted from The Open University and Trinity Guildhall Key Stage 2 Music CPD Programme.

## References

Booth, W. (1999) *For the Love of it*. Chicago: Chicago University Press.

Craft, A. (2005) *Creativity in Schools: Tensions and Dilemmas*. London: Routledge.

D'Amore, A. (ed.) (2009) *Musical Futures: An Approach to Teaching and Learning*. London: Paul Hamlyn Foundation.

Holt, J. (1977) *Instead of Education*. London: Pelican.

Jeffrey, B. and Woods, P. (2009) *Creative Learning in the Primary School*. London: Routledge.

Swanwick, K. (1999) *Teaching Music Musically*. London: Routledge.

# Chapter 12

# Realising creative development

*Philippa Bunting*

---

Children learn to talk by experimenting and listening; they can learn to make music by experimenting and listening – unless we stop them! Place children in surroundings that are full of 'invitations to learn', provide them with encouraging and sympathetic attitudes from adults as well as knowledge, and amazing things can happen – especially to the sensory perceptions that are central to the arts ... do we have the courage to embark with them on what are frequently unknown seas?

(Emma D. Sheehy in Acker 1990)

Imagination is more important than knowledge. For knowledge is limited to all we now know and understand, while imagination embraces the entire world, and all there ever will be to know and understand.

(Albert Einstein in Sheikh 1984)

## Introduction

Experimenting, listening and the exercise of imagination are three of the most exciting elements of learning in music, often providing the motivation for engaging with it in the first place.

Creative development, by which we mean the adoption of creative behaviours such as risk-taking, innovating, exploring, selecting and organising, and the development of creative ways of thinking and engaging, may well extend beyond the purely musical. The whole class instrumental/vocal setting provides a fertile opportunity for children to engage in new ways with this process.

By the end of this chapter we will have considered how creative work can become a natural part of whole class instrumental/vocal teaching (WCIVT) through teachers:

- fostering an environment in which creativity can flourish;
- establishing trust and respect in the creative classroom;
- facilitating flow in lessons;
- bringing together improvising, composing, listening and responding;
- making links with other art forms;
- recognising creative development.

## Fostering an environment in which creativity can flourish

Children are naturally creative, and inviting ideas from them will in almost all circumstances open the floodgates. What requires careful thought is how to support them in organising all the wonderful ideas that come pouring out. Teachers will need to consider how they might facilitate the development of creative behaviours and how to ensure that all voices – actual and musical – are heard, ensuring that the whole experience is not dominated by one or two strong personalities.

In the early stages, working creatively in music may involve manipulating already familiar musical material, using voices or instruments. Changing the words of a song or the pitches or rhythms of a piece of music, creating a series of variations exploring different textures and moods, making up a middle section to create a further piece in binary or ternary form, improvising ostinati and accompanying parts: all these build children's confidence with musical material and pave the way for future larger scale creative work. Working with music in this way demonstrates to children that music is there actively to be engaged with, not merely passively reproduced, and that they can be energetic explorers in, and skilful constructors of, their own musical landscape.

### Case study: Exploring a simple song

The children have learned a simple song about an apple tree, which they sing confidently. They transfer parts of the song to their instruments, starting with the melodic fragment associated with the word 'apple'. They then play around with this fragment, altering the pitch, rhythm and other musical features, gauging the effect of the changes and building up a bank of ideas. Then they start working on combining and overlaying these fragments. They discuss ideas of mood, thinking about who is singing this song, where and at what time of day.

The key features here are that the children are exploring: developing a confident relationship with a simple song, rolling their sleeves up and getting messy with the elements of music that they may later use as building blocks for their own musical creations. At this stage, responses are probably either individual, using a call and response structure, or collective, with the whole class trying out the ideas suggested.

As with all this type of work, the move to music making needs to be quick: there needs to be as much music and as little talk as possible. Work will be most successful where the teacher models creative behaviour – joining in the musical journey without seeking to influence it too much – and where the children have the opportunity to review and evaluate what they have done, enabling them to build on their creations on future occasions.

### Activity 12.1 Exploring the creative potential of simple materials

- Find, or compose, a simple song to provide a similar starting point for the type of work outlined in the above case study, perhaps one that makes a feature of names, places, animals, etc.
- Plan a lesson with your class which explores how the music associated with these words can be developed into rhythmic and then melodic fragments which could then be worked with creatively through being combined in a range of ways.
- Think about how you will support this work through modelling creative behaviours yourself.

## Establishing trust and respect in the creative classroom

The creative journey is one involving a good deal of trust and respect between teacher and pupils, teacher and other colleagues, and between the children themselves. It is important to establish ground rules from the start: in particular careful listening to, and respect for, everyone's contributions. All ideas should come from the children, with the teacher acting as facilitator. It is critical that teachers think carefully about how they respond to the contributions of children. Words such as 'good' or 'clever' imply arbitrary assessments which are ultimately unhelpful, whereas words such as 'interesting', 'exciting' and 'thoughtful' are less judgemental and can be used to support all children's offerings.

Praise should relate primarily to how children have responded to the music as it is being put together than to the inherent quality of the musical idea itself. Often the most productive ideas come from children with the least musical experience as they lack preconceptions that training often builds in, and are less likely to resort to the kind of 'musical clichés' that are quickly learned as they are inducted into particular styles or genres.

Remember to value every contribution and respond to it, or invite the children to do so. The skill of providing feedback that doesn't merely reflect personal taste and ideas is a useful one for life, and will swiftly build active listening skills.

---

*Case study: Using a counting system as a framework for creativity*

The children have been really taken with the idea of different counting systems, which they were introduced to in another lesson. As the school is in an area steeped in Celtic culture, the teacher suggests the system of five for counting sheep used by Birtwistle in his chamber opera *Yan Tan Tethera* as a starting point for creating a piece of music.

The introductory session starts with some physical actions combined in patterns of fives. It then moves on to a series of copycat activities, still using movement or sometimes vocalised, and still in five, but more expressive, such as:

| 1 | 2 | 3 | 4 | 5 |
|---|---|---|---|---|
| Knees | Nose | Tu- | -rn | Rest |
| Left | Right | Sh- | -i- | -mmy |
| Brrr- | -brrr | Rest | Rest | Bing! |

The children then clap or vocalise patterns within the structure of five, such as:

| 1 | 2 | 3 | 4 | 5 |
|---|---|---|---|---|
| Rest | Clap | Clap | Rest | Rest |
| Clap | Rest | Rest | Clap | Clap |

The children divide into groups and using their instruments and voices they support each other as they work with one of the patterns, sharing ideas and working creatively within the structure to produce a short improvisation. In the following weeks the work is extended in length and creatively in many ways, through:

- using different dynamics;
- building up to a climax and dramatic cut off;
- using children to 'conduct' the group, allowing them to build layers of each group's contribution in creative ways;
- adding vocal sounds or movement.

The teacher is careful with the language used in talking about the children's contributions, which gives them the confidence to experiment and take risks.

At first glance we might question how this case study models 'trust and respect'. The counting game offers children a starting point which is instantly accessible and where all can succeed, and this provides a context within which they feel secure. The children's creative input is small at the start but gradually increases in a supportive environment where their input is valued and respected. The case study demonstrates how trust and respect is not just about use of language but about all the ways we support learning.

---

*Activity 12.2 Fostering an environment of trust and respect*

- The counting system in the previous case study offered a framework for creative work. Think of another structure that you could use with your class in a similar way.
- How will you use this structure to provide an environment where everyone's contributions are valued?
- Think about what sort of language you will use, and encourage children to use, when discussing each other's contributions.

---

## Facilitating creative flow in the lesson

Creative work does not always proceed by logical steps, nor does it always come easily, particularly when independent working in groups introduces the need for sophisticated negotiating skills. Things can often get derailed by two things in particular: too much talking by the teacher, and individual children – often highly motivated and musically enthusiastic – who insist on trying out their own ideas to the detriment of the group dynamic.

In order to achieve a sense of flow in a large group or whole class environment, the teacher must be a skilful facilitator, setting the groups spinning like so many plates, whilst being on hand to intervene or nudge things forward. Interventions can be prompts to try all the ideas floating around, suggestions for ways to combine them, reminders that silence is also a powerful tool (compositions can quickly get very crowded when created collaboratively), listening to a performance of what has been suggested so far, and giving feedback.

Other tools at the teacher's disposal might include producing a set of cards with some ideas on, to push forward groups which have become stuck. These could take the form of words, simple pictures or even abstract shapes such as the ones in Figure 12.1.

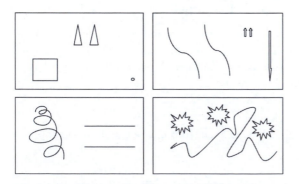

*Figure 12.1* Abstract shapes for musical creativity

Sometimes the most effective 'prompt' is a musical one where teachers join in with the children's music making, contributing their own ideas as one amongst equals.

Finally, whilst it might seem to militate against flow, it is a good idea to set a clear, short time limit for work before it is performed and feedback given both by the teacher and other pupils as this instils confidence by setting an expectation that children will create something worthy of listening to in a brief time.

The strategies outlined above have the potential to:

- engender an honest relationship to work in progress, showing that creativity is not something that happens behind closed doors and then emerges fully formed;
- initiate children into the idea that they are part of a community that encompasses the adults around them, and other creative artists they may have met;
- demand active and sensitive listening;
- give children a chance to develop their skills in describing musical work, responding to it, and providing constructive feedback.

One lurking pitfall in children's creative work is that it consists of no more than a series of sound effects, based on the most obvious features of the instrument, and that successive explorations produce similar results. In such a case, the children themselves will soon become dissatisfied if they cannot see that they are able to realise more advanced musical ideas.

There are many ways to work against this natural tendency, or rather to move things on from this natural starting point. If the focus throughout is on the quality of the output, of the actual sounds that are being produced and organised, this soon stops absent-minded doodling or inappropriate noises marring an otherwise engaging musical experience. If the teacher, acting as facilitator, also demonstrates willingness to join in and 'music' alongside the pupils, then the modelling provided is very valuable. Frequent listening to the work in progress, with constructive feedback from peers and from the teacher, provides opportunities for honing, and can also help raise the standard in the room to that of the most confident.

---

*Activity 12.3 Effective modelling and feedback*

Plan a short creative activity for your next whole class instrumental lesson where children will work in small groups to produce a short improvisation/composition based on one of the abstract shapes given in Figure 12.1. Consider carefully how you will:

- use your own musical skills to model the activity and to support the children as they work on their music;
- frame your own and other children's feedback so that it is supportive and enables the children to make further progress.

---

## Bringing together improvising, composing, listening and responding

In a previous section we referred to the idea of how 'getting messy with the elements of music' provides an ideal context for creative behaviour. It is difficult to engage with musical materials in this way whilst maintaining distinctions between musical roles of listener, improviser and performer. Rather it implies engaging with all the activities which constitute what it is to be musical – composing/improvising, performing and listening in an integrated way. Listening, however, is the key element in all musical activity. Learning to listen attentively and critically is a skill learners will develop as they work on their own ideas, and respond to those of their peers. It can easily and naturally be extended to involve listening to existing works, responding to them both verbally and in music. Listening is important not just in relation to the children's own work, however, but also so they can hear how other musicians have responded to various stimuli, and to experience new sound worlds.

---

### Case study: Using Haydn's Surprise Symphony as a creative stimulus

The children listen to the opening of the *Andante* from Haydn's *Surprise Symphony*. They identify what the element of surprise is, and perform it either with the recording (if their instruments are at an appropriate pitch) or using another form of accompaniment provided by the teacher.

They go on to discuss other ways in which the element of surprise might be introduced into a piece of music and how musical expectations are set up and then confounded. They include ideas such as sudden dramatic silences, quick changes from one texture to another, or a repeated pattern which alters at a given signal.

Working in small groups they explore some of these ideas, creating short pieces to illustrate them. They then perform to one another without identifying the 'surprise' element, instead asking their peers to listen out for it and identify it for themselves.

---

### Activity 12.4 Using recorded music as a stimulus for creativity

- Select a piece of recorded music with a strong, identifiable musical feature to act as a stimulus for creative activity.
- Discuss with your class what impact the musical feature has and how it does it.
- Support the children to work in small groups on different ways of achieving a similar impact.

---

## Embracing other art forms

Although narrative is not always the most musical starting point, it can help children extend their work, and can also provide a useful framework for linking together disparate ideas which develop in small group work in the context of WCIVT. A character can be created to link the journey together and a child chosen to lead the performance, either acting out the journey or 'conducting' it. The children could produce a series of artworks to represent the different stages which could then be used as a form of score. There is plenty of scope here for discussing emotion and timbre as the character passes through, say, a spiky forest, over stepping stones, through the grounds of a scary castle …

Children could also be involved in providing a sound track to a short film sequence, though this will need careful work to guide it away from mere sound effects into a more musical response to the action seen. Something quite abstract is better than an action sequence where they will hear in their heads the kind of highly produced music they are used to on television or in the cinema. Children working at different levels can be given different sections to work on, perhaps responding to copies of stills from the film, with the more experienced taking responsibility for the more complex or extended sequences. In this scenario the teacher can really be involved as a musician, providing linking material and helping the children realise their ambitions.

---

### Case study: Whole class instrumental group work with a Kandinsky painting

Working from a painting by Kandinsky, the children first decide whether they are going to respond to it as a whole, or take discrete parts to work into music. They decide whether to produce something which gives an 'all at once' impression of the picture, or a piece which follows a narrative journey through the artwork, dwelling on particular features, or moving from the edges to the middle, or following the eyes as they dwell first on one feature then another. They decide what features of contrast there are, and whether any of the features exist in dramatic relationship to one another.

As they work, they are building up the kind of relationship with the picture that they will eventually have with the music they create in response to it, coming to know it as one knows a familiar face.

In future lessons they develop the music further, perhaps exploring ways of representing what they are doing musically through their own artwork, perhaps through making marks which reflect the kind of sounds they are making as a form of invented notation. They may then move on to playing their own pictures rather than the Kandinsky which was the original stimulus.

---

## Recognising creative development

In the kind of activities proposed in this chapter, no single one is particularly suited to beginners, or to more advanced players, as all can be accessed at the level of experience the children are at. In any one activity the range of outcomes will be hugely diverse.

Moving from initial playful engagement, which children will almost certainly have already experienced in other areas, if not music, creative development is perhaps most usefully seen as proceeding by means of increasing:

- confidence;
- control;
- expressiveness;
- ability to match actual to imagined musical effects;
- sensitivity to context;
- critical awareness;
- ability to reflect upon one's own work and that of others;
- ability to evaluate, and to describe the results of that evaluation with increasing confidence and discernment.

Many would argue that complexity should be another factor which increases, but if the musical effect desired is one of simplicity, then complexity for its own sake could be seen as retrogressive. For this reason it is excluded from the list above, but can of course be taken into consideration.

## Conclusion

In the QCA document *Creativity: Find it, Promote it* (2004) certain characteristics of creative thinking and behaviour are identified:

- Questioning and challenging conventions and assumptions.
- Making inventive connections and associating things that are not usually related.
- Envisaging what might be: imagining – seeing things in the mind's eye.
- Trying alternatives and fresh approaches, keeping options open.
- Reflecting critically on ideas, actions and outcomes.

Thinking of music in particular, it is easy to map these ideas onto the kind of work proposed above:

- Questioning musical conventions, developing the confidence to manipulate and reorganise existing musical materials, and using them as the basis for improvisation in a spirit of playful exploration.
- Combining new sounds and using a wide range of stimuli to compose music which can then be organised or recombined in innovative ways.
- Hearing musical results inwardly, then working to realise them in sound using instruments and voices.
- The use of open-ended tasks (particularly harmonically) allows for a wide range of musical responses.
- Frequent performances of work in progress give the opportunity to discuss its musical effectiveness, and to provide positive feedback.

Musically creative classrooms are noisy places, like workshops full of sound. But the benefits in terms of engagement, the development of critical listening and the providing of intrinsic motivation to develop one's own relationship with music, with the instrument, with one's own musical and creative voice, are enormous. As children develop their confidence as generators and performers of their own music, learning to ally imagination with increasing experience, they will become independent musicians who are motivated by, and take responsibility for, their own learning. They will truly become active creators of their own musical meaning, operating in new, challenging and positive spaces, and embarking, together with their teachers, on those 'frequently unknown seas'.

## References

Acker, G. (1990) *Music Quotes* (www.the-improvisor.com/muquotes.html).
QCA (2004) *Creativity: Find it, Promote it*. London: QCA.
Sheikh, A. (1984) *Imagination and Healing* (Baywood Publishing Company) or http://thinkexist.com/quotes/albert_einstein.

## Further reading

Koestler, A. (1964) *The Art of Creation*. London: Allen and Unwin.
Mills, J. (2005) *Music in the School*. Oxford: Oxford University Press.
Nahmanovitch, S. (1991) *Free Play: The Power of Improvisation in Life and the Arts*. New York: Jeremy P. Tarcher/Penguin.
Swanwick, K. (1999) *Teaching Music Musically*. London: Routledge.

## Resources

www.musicalfutures.org.uk
www.soundjunction.org

# Part 5

# Collaboration
## Setting the scene

*Julie Evans*

In simple terms, collaboration means working together. Collaboration is particularly important in terms of whole class instrumental and vocal teaching (WCIVT) because any music making in a large ensemble relies on a variety of collaborations. When different agencies collaborate to develop children's musical learning experiences these will also be integrated to a greater or lesser extent and the chapters on collaboration link closely to those about integration. When considering whole class instrumental and vocal teaching and learning, it is important to establish who might be working together and how collaboration can be as effective as possible.

Because whole classes of pupils are going to be learning to play or sing it is likely that there will be an impact on the whole school, not only in terms of practicalities such as resourcing but also on the musical life of the school. It is imperative that the headteacher and senior management of a school fully support the teaching and learning and will collaborate with all practitioners. This might mean facilitating important essentials such as changes to the curriculum and timetabling of space as well as establishing and maintaining what Southworth, Nias and Campbell (in Pollard 2002: 349) call a 'culture of collaboration'. These authors suggest that a school's culture of collaboration is built on four interacting beliefs:

- valuing individuals – as people and for their contribution to others;
- valuing interdependence – belonging to a group and working as a team;
- valuing security;
- valuing openness.

It is the valuing of interdependence that is key to establishing and maintaining effective collaboration. In schools with a 'culture of collaboration' Southworth, Nias and Campbell observe:

> Individual staff members ... valued one another as people, each with his/her identity, personality, interests, skills, experiences and potential. Yet they also appreciated the diversity which this brought to the school. Likewise, interdependence has two aspects. Together the members of ... staff made a group that was valued because it provided a sense of belonging. At the same time they accepted a collective responsibility for the work of the school so creating a sense of team in which staff helped, encouraged and substituted for one another.
>
> (Pollard 2002: 350)

These can be suggested as the conditions for effective collaboration. An effective 'culture of collaboration' may already exist within a school but whole class instrumental teaching and learning will mean that the collaborative community will be extended beyond the existing staff of the school. It is very likely that the whole class teaching will be led by a 'specialist' practitioner who is not a member of the school's existing staff. This practitioner might be an instrumental or vocal teacher from a music service, a self-employed teacher, a community musician or workshop leader. This practitioner will clearly bring 'his/her identity, personality, interests, skills, experiences and potential' to the school. These may be very different to that of the pupils' usual class teacher but this should be regarded as a strength rather than a problem in the view of Southworth *et al.* (op. cit.).

It is intended that whole class instrumental and vocal teaching should be an integrated experience for pupils. This means that the class teachers will need to be fully involved in the learning process, learning alongside pupils. This will ensure that the instrumental and vocal learning is not a 'bolt on' but is fully related to the pupils' curriculum music. In some schools learning support assistants have also been fully involved in whole class instrumental and vocal learning, to good effect. As Glover and Young point out, 'If it is a belief within a school that music is for all children, then it must be borne out among the adults in the school also' (Glover and Young 1998: 7). Such a model allows for collaboration between visiting musicians, class teachers *and* support staff.

As collaboration extends beyond the school, it will allow pupils' wider musical interests to be embraced within the collaborative model. This joined-up experience is very positive for pupils: 'If a school can establish a musical ethos which is alive in its response to the range of music children encounter beyond the school in the wider community, the quality of children's musical experience and learning is very much enhanced' (Glover and Young 1998: 5).

This collaboration between practitioners within and beyond the school is a two-way process. Pupils will be able to take their experience from school into their communities. For instance, pupils might be able to perform in a community arts festival. Conversely, pupils will be able to bring their musical experience outside of school *into* the school. For instance, a pupil might have gained experience as a tabla player or gospel singer within their community and this experience must be capitalised on within the school. It is also important to develop collaboration in order to make real links for the pupils between their whole class instrumental and vocal learning and their learning within the curriculum. For instance, pupils can use their developing instrumental and vocal skills when they are composing.

All of these models of collaboration require practitioners to devote a great deal of time to planning to ensure that the pupils' musical learning is effective. The practitioners will need to negotiate in order to establish clear shared aims and objectives. They will need to consider different models of collaborative teaching, such as:

- one practitioner leads and the others support;
- one practitioner leads and the others work with a specific group of pupils (e.g. gifted and talented pupils; pupils with special needs);
- each practitioner takes responsibility for particular parts of the session;
- all practitioners work together, seamlessly taking over responsibility when appropriate or performing together to model to pupils.

Finally, it is imperative that pupils are also given opportunities to work collaboratively. Bruner states:

I have come increasingly to recognise that most learning in most settings is a communal activity, a sharing of culture. It is not just that the child must make his knowledge his own, but he must make it his own in the community of those who share his sense of belonging to a culture.

(Bruner 1986: 127)

In the first chapter in this section Tim Palmer (with Julie Evans and Gary Spruce) will discuss collaboration with partners beyond the school. In the following chapter Rita Burt will consider how two or more teachers can adopt a collaborative approach to planning and what this planning might involve.

## References

Bruner, J. (1986) *Actual Minds: Possible Worlds*. Cambridge, MA: Harvard Educational Press.
Glover, J. and Young, S. (1998) *Primary Music: Later Years*. London: Routledge.
Pollard, A. (ed.) (2002) *Readings for Reflective Teaching*. London: Continuum.

Chapter 13

# Collaborative music teaching and learning with partners beyond the school

*Tim Palmer with Julie Evans and Gary Spruce*

## Introduction

Working with partners with different backgrounds and from a wide range of teaching experiences and contexts can be enriching and rewarding for all those involved. In this chapter we will focus particularly on how collaborations between schools and visiting artists and arts organisations can enrich children's music education. We will also consider the impact of such collaborations on the professional practice of teachers and visiting artists particularly in the context of whole class instrumental and vocal teaching (WCIVT). We will look at the value and practicalities of such partnerships and how all those involved can gain the most from them.

By the end of this chapter we will have considered the following questions:

*   What are the potential benefits of collaborations with partners beyond the school?
*   What conditions need to be in place for successful collaborations to happen?
*   What kinds of collaboration might be established and how?

## What are the potential benefits of collaborations with partners beyond the school?

Collaborations and partnerships are no longer a bolt-on luxury but a key foundational element of a successful learning environment. Learning is itself a partnership activity, infused with resonances that remain indelibly associated with the skills or knowledge learnt – resonances of relationships, emotions and contexts. As John-Steiner puts it:

> An individual learns, creates and achieves mastery in and through his or her relationships with other individuals. Ideas, tools and processes that emerge from joint activity are appropriated, or internalized, by the individual and become the basis of the individual's subsequent development.
>
> (John-Steiner 2000: 5)

Personal knowledge and understanding – both musical and pedagogical – are recognised here as co-constructed and resulting from social interaction. It is important therefore to recognise that collaborative working has the potential to impact – positively or negatively – on all those involved.

Later in this chapter, we will consider the conditions that need to be in place to ensure that collaborations are positive and beneficial experiences for all. Before this, however, we will explore the potential gains for schools who work with visiting artists in the music classroom.

### Reconnecting with the musical community

By their very presence in the musical classroom, visiting musicians (be they professional musicians or musicians from within the community) create a *reconnection* with pupils' music making outside of school. In some instances this reconnection will be with the music making that children are already involved in within their communities, in other instances with the wider musical world.

There has historically been a disconnection between school music and that in which pupils are involved in the community – church groups, brass bands or family music making, for example – and opportunities need to be found for pupils to make such connections, both musically or socially, for example having a joint workshop, sharing a concert platform. Because of their mixed age groups, varied repertoire and 'real-world' settings these ensembles often have a high validity amongst participating children, and often set high expectations. These reconnections, be they with community groups, symphony orchestras, rock musicians or new music organisations, have, in the words of Everitt, the potential to contribute to the '[retrieval] of a lost sense of community' (1997: 100) – a sense of community which has the potential to develop a shared vision and set of values for music education.

---

#### Activity 13.1 Contacting musicians in your area

Find out who the practising musicians in your local area are. Make a list of any ensembles or individuals that regularly perform locally, within any genre. Contact the musician(s) to set up a performance that could stimulate a group composition with your WCIVT group.
  For instance:

- a rock band might play a number based on a bass riff resulting in a composition using a repeated bass line;
- a folk musician might sing or play a piece based on a pentatonic scale resulting in a composition using a pentatonic scale or just a couple of notes from a pentatonic scale;
- a string quartet might play a piece which uses extended techniques resulting in a composition where pupils make sounds using their instruments and/or voices in unconventional (but not harmful) ways.

---

Negotiate with the musicians about what they can offer your pupils. As well as simply performing to pupils, the musicians might get them to use their own instruments/voices copying what they model. They could let pupils try out instruments that they have never seen before to understand a little about how they work. Pupils might compose a piece to perform in a future session. (This could be presented by the pupils as a graphic score or a lead sheet.)

Use the first session to develop your pupils' audience skills. This might include them learning about listening appropriately (e.g. without talking in some cases). Encourage your pupils to formulate questions to ask the musicians (e.g. about the possible pitch range of their instruments, what extended techniques can be achieved without damaging the instruments). Ensure that the performance session is not an isolated one-off occasion but is prepared for, and leads on to, other work.

### Bringing particular musical skills

Although some classroom teachers may not have had formal musical training, it is important not to characterise them as being in some way 'non-musical'. It is true, however, that visiting, expert musicians can bring to the classroom particular musical knowledge and skills which the classroom teacher may not possess. Even a classroom teacher who is an experienced musician cannot hope to have the knowledge and understanding required to be able to teach with confidence across the breadth and range of styles, genres and traditions of today's musical world. Indeed there are dangers in attempting to do so particularly in respect of unfamiliar musical traditions and cultures. As Adams says:

> When teaching any musical tradition consideration had to be given to the context in which the tradition is celebrated, and care taken about a possible 'tokenistic' approach, which may not do justice to the music itself nor respect the musical experiences of its cultural origins.
>
> (Adams 2007: 255)

It is in contexts such as these where a visiting musician with a particular background which enables him/her to acknowledge such sensitivities or simply brings an extra dimension to the teacher's expertise can be of immense value.

### Musical authenticity

Visiting musicians can bring a musical 'authenticity' to the classroom. They often have a 'oneness' with the tradition within which they make music and with the instruments they play, and an uninhibited engagement around playing that pupils rapidly learn to mimic. They demonstrate what Swanwick refers to as 'musical fluency', fluency that is particularly evident amongst musicians who do not use notation; primarily musicians from outside the Western classical tradition where there is 'the aural ability to image music coupled with the skill of handling an instrument (or voice) that characterises jazz, Indian music, rock music, music for steel-pans, a great deal of computer assisted music and folk music anywhere in the world' (Swanwick 1999: 56).

### Different approaches to musical teaching and learning

Visiting musicians will bring to the classroom pedagogies that are embedded and reflected in the musical tradition and culture within which they make music and these can contrast with and add breadth to the strategies already in place. These pedagogies might include an aural approach to musical learning or one in which improvisation is a key element. It is important to recognise, however, that, depending upon the experience and skills of these musicians as teachers, such pedagogies might be implicit rather than explicit and it is the key role here of the expert teacher to frame and support the musician in making explicit these pedagogies to further children's musical learning. Pitts puts this well when she speaks of classroom teachers as being 'ideally positioned to act as skilled co-ordinators for practitioners in the art world, whose distinctive perspectives might add a welcome new dimension to young people's musical learning' (Pitts 2007: 768).

> *Activity 13.2 Making connections with arts organisations*
>
> Arrange to talk with schools or arts organisations about the kinds of collaborative events they have been involved in. Try and go and observe part of one of these 'in action'. Think about the extent to which it provides, or would provide, the benefits outlined above and any changes you might want to make to it to enhance its effectiveness for your own context.

Effective and rich collaborations will provide opportunities for learning by all those involved. Through working with children in schools, visiting musicians are given the space and opportunity to re-examine their own beliefs about music and musical learning which then has an impact on their own practice as a musician. Orchestral musicians, for example, can over time become straitjacketed by the constant suppression of personal interpretation, and an over-reliance upon 'notation to sound' transfer that bypasses a personalisation of the music. By engaging with the habits of animateur activity, aural learning, highly communicative leadership and breaking down repertoire into constituent components, visiting artists can develop their critical faculties in relation to their own music making. This can in turn feed back into more risk-taking and livelier and more informed performances throughout a career. Working with children can also cause musicians to reassess their own beliefs about the nature of music and musical creativity and the value of young people's creative products.

## What conditions need to be in place for successful collaborations to happen?

Successful collaborations do not just happen. They need to be planned and the conditions put in place for their successful implementation. They also need to be underpinned by a coherent philosophy of what effective music learning is and the way in which it can be brought about through collaborative working.

Successful collaborations fulfil at least some of the following conditions and characteristics.

### *Mutual respect for the understanding, skills and knowledge that each person brings to the partnership*

Successful collaborations are underpinned by a mutual respect amongst all those involved. In order to develop effective collaborations, it is important that those working together do not fall back on stereotypical models of what each might bring to children's musical learning: typically that the visiting musician will bring the musical skills and the classroom teacher the pedagogical and management strategies. Teachers may well be practising musicians themselves. Everyone will bring to their role an implicit musical understanding gained simply from the role of music in their own lives – their own musical enculturation.

As we have already established, visiting musicians may promote (implicitly or explicitly) musical practices that articulate new pedagogical approaches, and experienced animateurs will have a developed understanding of the ways in which children can be enthused to make music and ways in which they learn best. Successful collaborations will provide opportunities to develop all aspects of each partner's professional practice.

> ### Activity 13.3 Collaborative working and professional development
>
> What do you feel are your strengths in relation to pedagogy and musical practice and what might you want to develop in both these areas as a result of a collaborative project? Who might you work with, and what kinds of collaborative working would support you in achieving your professional development aims?

### Agreed aims and approaches

Effective collaborations are characterised by a shared vision of what is to be achieved and approaches to realising this vision that are negotiated and agreed upon. The developing and sharing of this vision can be one of the most professionally rewarding and creative aspects of collaborative working. Where there is mutual respect for each other, a secure environment is created within which ideas can be shared without being fully formed but then picked up and developed by others. Collaborative working is, as was noted in the introductory chapter to this section, about:

- valuing individuals – as people and for their contribution to others;
- valuing interdependence – belonging to a group and working as a team;
- valuing security;
- valuing openness.

Apart from developing a shared musical and educational vision for the project, it is also important that there is an agreed set of working practices. Visiting musicians will be aware that each school has its own protocols and expectations relating to the management of learning and lesson planning whilst the musician will have particular ways of working that are tested and which s/he has confidence in. These need to be accommodated. Talking with each other about these is critically important to the development of effective working relationships:

> Talk about your approach to behaviour and classroom management, talk about the kind of language you will both use to reward and encourage, talk about pace and rhythm of sessions and how you'll manage those, talk about timekeeping and planning, and make sure you've made a viable plan for meeting to review progress.
>
> (Deane and Zeserson 2008: 9–10)

### Evaluation and review

Part of the initial planning for any collaborative project should be how its success will be evaluated and reviewed. Reviewing and evaluating should be an ongoing process and should be made not only against the planned milestones and outcomes but also against those unexpected outcomes that emerge from all *musical* interactions. This constant process of reviewing and evaluating will ensure that the project has an initial focus and remains focused.

It is particularly important to be able to demonstrate to the school community (children, other teachers and headteachers), parents, funding bodies and arts organisations how successful the project has been so as to strengthen the case for future support for collaborative working. Teachers in school will demonstrate how the project has connected both with the wider curriculum and the music curriculum in terms of providing enrichment. They also need to be able to show how the project has contributed to the wider life of the school. Visiting musicians are likely to be asked to demonstrate how the project and its outcomes have contributed to the aims of their organisation.

Demonstrating such impact through evaluation and review is not easy. As Adams says, both visiting musicians and teachers 'face similar challenges ... when trying to evaluate and measure the success of project outcomes, that is they find qualitative measures "much harder to agree" than quantative' (Adams 2007: 259). However, it is important that such challenges do not cause those involved to resort to demonstrating impact exclusively through extra-musical factors (e.g. through impact on literacy scores or attendance) and thereby to ignore the very rationale for the project – the development and enrichment of children's musical learning and experiences. Audio and video recordings are particularly useful here and should be used not just to provide evidence of the final 'product' but also the journey that the teachers and children have undergone – the progress that has been made in both children's musical learning and musicians' and teachers' professional practices.

### Planning for a legacy

Finally, each project should leave a legacy that sustains and enthuses all those who have taken part – particularly the children – to develop further their professional practice, musical learning and experience. Teachers and musicians will take away from successful collaborative projects new ways of working and new musical and pedagogical understandings. For the children, however, what is of most importance is the quality of the project's music making. Zeserson put this well when she writes:

> Making excellent music with others – adults or young people – is a joyous experience that affirms community. Your pupils will remember this feeling long after the detail of the programme fades from the memory, and the values of inclusion, respect and mutual achievement that underpins great music making will stay with them for life.
>
> (Zeserson 2009: 89)

## What kinds of collaboration might be established and how?

Outside the immediate school context, there are many possible individuals or organisations with whom a partnership could be very productive for all concerned. Most performing organisations that are in receipt of public money have a widening participation agenda, and will have education departments. Whilst the many orchestras in the UK are an obvious choice, musical partners could also include choirs, theatre companies, jazz or pop musicians, chamber ensembles, traditional music ensembles from many cultures, or individual freelance performers.

These opportunities are not only available in large cities, as a number of community music organisations exist to make links between artists and hosts in rural areas: some of the Youth Music Action Zones fill this brief, for example. Additionally, the visiting artists that might collaborate with your school might be semi-professional or amateur musicians. A local folk singer-songwriter might support whole class singing, for example, and a partnership could offer many significant benefits, not least as a role model.

Many university music departments and conservatoires have outreach programmes placing projects or student helpers into schools. Performing arts centres and venues are also working on ways of building an audience and justifying public subsidy through schools' work, and can offer exciting performance venues as well. Cross-curricular visits to other sites (museums or art galleries, for example) can provide exciting stimuli for compositions.

---

### Case study: Music and dance

A primary school in South-East London has had a project running for four years in partnership with both Trinity College of Music and Laban Centre of Contemporary Dance (now TrinityLaban), initially funded by Creative Partnerships. Exploring the links between music and dance, two Year 5 classes spend half a term working to a common stimulus, with one class creating the music for the other's dance choreography, before swapping roles for the second half of term. Initially led by visiting artists, the project included a strong element of CPD, and is now led by the school teacher, with artistic advice only from the two Higher Education Institutions (HEIs), along with placements by PGCE students. HEIs often engage well with their local education context, but it is rare to find a project that is self-sustaining in such a positive way, offering training placements back to the music college.

---

It is important to realise that the quality and the musical intentions of visiting musicians need to be evaluated in advance of any partnership. For instance, a visiting individual musician may be an excellent practitioner but may not have developed extensive pedagogical skills. Equally, organisations such as orchestras may have demands made upon them to carry out educational projects and these may not always be underpinned by the same ideologies as those held by classroom teachers who are working with pupils on a daily basis. Instrument makers are also often proactive in their relationships with schools: Yamaha and Roland are notable in this respect. Such organisations will obviously have an agenda to sell instruments and may promote a certain methodology of instrumental learning which may be quite prescriptive, but they can offer schools support, for instance in their online facilities.

It is equally important, of course, for schools to develop partnerships with organisations that will not just affirm their approach to music education but that might challenge them to think their practices anew or provide a means of addressing a particularly intransigent problem. For example, a school might develop a partnership with an organisation or practitioner that has expertise in encouraging boys to sing or including children that play non-orchestral instruments in the musical life of the school. Whatever the reason for within to enter into a partnership with an external organisation or musicians, it is advisable to look into the kinds of projects that they have already been involved in and the particular perspectives, vision and ideologies which underpin their work.

---

### Activity 13.4 Evaluating potential partners

Enquire about relevant publications by any music organisations or funding partners that your school has contact with. Do they have evaluation reports from earlier projects that document learning processes that could be applicable to you? What problems have others encountered that you can learn to avoid as you plan partnerships? Are there any wider themes that have or could be developed? Funding bodies often put up evaluations on their websites.

One often overlooked partner in children's arts learning is the family. It can play a role as a provider of skills, with talented parents performing or assisting learning; as a nurturing supporter of personal practice (although parents often need help in learning how to support their children in this way); and as a motivating force, by taking children to external concerts or workshops, or facilitating their staying late after school for ensembles or additional activities. Schools that have managed to engage parents effectively and in an appropriately targeted manner increase the likelihood of pupils continuing and developing their musical activities.

---

*Activity 13.5 Involving parents*

Think about how a school currently engages parental support for music, and how this can be developed. Could parents be invited to a whole class instrumental lesson to learn how to support practice? Could they assist in an extra-curricular ensemble, either by playing or by helping with practicalities? There might even be an opportunity to set up a class for parent-learners after school, and a school community orchestra!

---

## Conclusion

By grasping the opportunities afforded in this connected world, pupils, staff, visiting teachers, partner schools and communities can all collaborate to bring excitement, enjoyment, opportunity and diversity to children's music making. WCIVT can mark a shift in attitudes – to participation, to learning, to music and to other cultures. The list of possible partners is endless – performances can take place across the internet to other schools in different parts of the world, and partnerships can be established with online resource providers.

Collaborative learning is *exciting* learning and, if closely linked to good relationships, a stimulating environment and a supportive context, then collaboration plays a key role in inspiring success. There are challenges, however, not least those presented by schools that are focused on meeting the external demands of a 'standards-driven agenda' to resist outside 'distractions' and also the way in which visiting musicians can sometimes appear to give the impression that they alone have the key to the secret garden of good practice. As Pitts argues:

> ... greater effort is needed to ensure compatibility and cooperation ... through systematic evaluation of their distinctive roles in music teaching and learning. Only with this increased understanding of the links between music in schools, informal learning, and the outreach projects that bridge that gap, can music classrooms truly become vibrant places of cultural exchange and musical engagement.
>
> (op. cit.: 771)

## References

Adams, P. (2007) 'Beyond the classroom 2: Collaborative partnerships', in C. Philpott and G. Spruce (eds) *Learning to Teach Music in the Secondary School: A Companion to School Experience*. London: Routledge.

Deane, K. and Zeserson, K. (2008) *Music in the Wider Community*. London: The Open University and Trinity College, London, Key Stage 2 Continuing Professional Development Programme.

Everitt, A. (1997) *Joining In: An Investigation into Participatory Music.* London: Calouste Gulbenkian Foundation.

John-Steiner, V. (2000) *Creative Collaboration.* Oxford: Oxford University Press.

Pitts, S. (2007) 'Music beyond school', in L. Bresler (ed.) *International Handbook of Research in Arts Education.* Dordecht, The Netherlands: Springer.

Swanwick, K. (1999) *Teaching Music Musically.* London: Routledge.

Zeserson, K. (2009) 'Musical collaborations with other adults', in J. Evans and C. Philpott (eds) *A Practical Guide to Teaching Music in the Secondary School.* London: Routledge.

# Chapter 14

# A collaborative approach to planning, teaching and learning

*Rita Burt*

## Introduction

Collaboration is at the heart of successful whole class instrumental and vocal teaching. The professionals who work together might be instrumental teachers, classroom teachers or visiting community musicians – they will all bring their own skills and approaches, but when they work together in a co-ordinated way the effect can be dramatic. A central recommendation in *Music Manifesto Report No. 2: Making Every Child's Music Matter* (DfES 2006) is that 'everyone involved in music education should work together to provide a framework and focus needed to deliver a universal music education' (ibid.: 7). Initiatives such as Musical Futures,[1] whole class instrumental and vocal programmes (WCIVT) or Wider Opportunities and many educational outreach projects involving teachers, musicians and orchestras have placed increasing emphasis on class teachers, music teachers, performers and community musicians working together. Working with partners with different musical backgrounds and from a wide range of teaching experiences and contexts can be enriching and rewarding for practitioners and children alike.

The success and impact of working in this way depends to a large extent on how well collaborating partners work together. Collaborative planning and teaching is all about *working together*. This can take different forms but, whatever the model, its effectiveness will be dependent upon all those involved developing an agreed and shared approach to teaching and learning. Establishing effective working relationships and developing collaborative models which make the best of your collective skills and experiences is central to successful collaborative practice. Such relationships support the cross-fertilisation of teaching and musical skills and experiences which is invaluable to both practitioners and children. Musical horizons are broadened and pedagogy strengthened whilst children benefit from the breadth, diversity and exposure to a range of role models and different approaches.

By the end of this chapter we will have considered the following questions:

- What are the characteristics and benefits of different models of collaborative planning and teaching?
- Who might work together?
- What perspectives might these partners bring and how might these enhance the quality of music teaching and learning?
- How might we create and develop successful collaborations?

## What are the characteristics and benefits of different models of collaborative planning and teaching?

Each new partnership is about developing a relationship of equals, and therefore models of collaborative teaching are about finding ways to match and develop the skills and experiences each participant brings. The starting point requires models which both reflect the teaching team's current expertise and confidence whilst at the same time supporting team and individual development which enable all to contribute equally.

In the 'Setting the scene' chapter for this section, Julie Evans identifies four models of collaborative teaching which can be seen as progressive (see Table 14.1).

*Table 14.1* Models of collaboration

| Model 1 | Model 2 | Model 3 | Model 4 |
|---|---|---|---|
| One practitioner leads and the others support | One practitioner leads and others work with specific groups of pupils (e.g. gifted and talented, pupils with special needs) | Each practitioner takes responsibility for particular parts of the session | All practitioners work together, seamlessly taking over responsibility when appropriate |

The first model, where one practitioner leads and others support, might be an appropriate place to start in some circumstances where less confident or less experienced practitioners are involved, allowing the more experienced or music specialist to lead. However, where opportunities are provided for the teacher to move away from the supporting role, then this model may be effective in supporting the development of future lead teachers. It may well be that one of the planned outcomes is to move to a way of working where all feel able to contribute more equally.

The second model, where one practitioner leads and others have specific support roles, provides opportunities to support different groups of pupils. The limitations of this model occur when roles are fixed (as in some examples of the first model) rather than being rotated.

The third model, where each practitioner takes responsibility for planned activities or sections of lessons, allows each to take a lead role at some point. The division of labour in this way needs to be carefully planned so as to avoid a sense of fragmentation or lack of pace and flow. However, when planned well, this 'patchwork quilt' approach can work well and can provide a stepping stone towards the fourth model.

The fourth model is the ideal to which we should strive and aspire and often develops from the third model. Here all practitioners work together, seamlessly taking over responsibility when appropriate. This model relies upon agreed and understood learning objectives and outcomes and a pedagogy which is shared and developed by all. It offers a flexible, creative and responsive approach to teaching which, when experienced, is fluid and organic without losing its direction or purpose.

Whichever model is adopted, it is vital that the professionals involved have time to plan work together. Time for joint planning and discussion is key to effective collaboration and without it teams of teachers will struggle to move beyond the first model.

---

*Activity 14.1 Reflecting on your own collaborative working*

Consider which of these models reflects your current practice and whether your experience of it reflects the above analysis of its strengths and weaknesses. What do you feel that you need to do to move your practice and that of your colleagues to the ideal of the fourth model?

## Who might work together?

Music education collaborations can be inspiring, enriching and rewarding for all involved. Whole class instrumental and vocal teaching (WCIVT) has brought a new focus for collaboration, with a common model being one where the classroom teacher and visiting instrumental specialist work together. Historically, community musicians, orchestral education outreach programmes, ensembles and music education organisations locally and nationally have worked with schools and young people to enhance their musical landscape. These partnership projects have tended to focus on workshop-type activity where all children participate and experience music making through composing and performing, typically around a specific musical genre or tradition. Often these are organised or brokered by local music services or arts services who have developed relationships or links with a wide network of professional musicians/organisations in order to support musical learning locally and are generally one-off or short-term projects. The longer-term collaborative relationship that underpins WCIVT is a relatively new development and requires a sustained approach to joint planning for musical learning. The opportunities for live performance in a range of possible genres, traditions or styles are dependent on the musician/instrumental tutors involved and what expertise they bring to the programme.

Many musicians have a wide portfolio which includes both performing and educational work, are experienced at leading educational workshops, and engage in instrumental teaching too. Some schools have teachers who are musicians amongst their own staff who are willing and able to support music collaborations. Additionally some local authorities provide additional specialist input to support and maximise these opportunities for the children's musical learning. An example of this is the following.

*Case study: Incorporating African music into WCIVT*

A primary school is planning a term-long project about the African continent and culture for Years 5 and 6 for the summer term. They liaise with the music service to discuss what input or resources might be available to support this. The music service has links with a gospel vocal leader locally, has a Ghanaian djembe teacher on their team and can also recommend a jazz trio with a strong educational background who could focus on African Township music. The school plan the music curriculum for both years around these three musical foci and find the common musical features such as singing, improvisation, riffs and ostinati, call and response, and copy back. A coherent programme is set up, with live musicians supporting through workshop events planned at various points in the term. Links with other subjects are also explored and planned. This programme culminates with a week of workshops with all three musicians/groups, leading to performances for the whole school and parents.

*Activity 14.2 Collaborative working and musical genres and traditions*

Choose a musical genre or tradition which you and your colleagues wish to introduce into your lessons. Explore the characteristics of the music and then consider:

1   the musical practices of the culture from which the music comes, i.e. how the music is created, performed, disseminated and received;
2   what particular kinds of musical learning and understanding the practices and music of this tradition/culture help to promote;
3   how the music might contribute to children's musical and cultural understanding.

## What perspectives might these partners bring and how might these enhance the quality of music teaching and learning?

Every person – teacher or performer – has differing perspectives, experience, approaches and skills to bring to collaborative planning and teaching. The challenge is for partners to support and learn from each other through recognising what each brings to the teaching context and to exploit and develop their specific areas of expertise so that children benefit from the range and breadth of experience which the team brings. Collaborative work at its best thrives on this diversity of approach. The aim should be to nurture and develop and to ensure that we do not marginalise those who may lack confidence, ambition or specific expertise. Recognising and valuing what practitioners from different contexts bring to children's musical learning and experience is central to establishing effective collaborative programmes and team work.

All musicians and instrumental teachers may inspire children through their performing and provide excellent role models, whilst the class or school teacher brings a wealth of understanding about the pedagogy of the classroom, prior musical learning and the children's needs and interests. *Making More of Music* (Ofsted 2009) states: 'Schools can contribute as much to developing the instrumental teachers' teaching skills as the instrumental teachers can bring to a school's overall music provision' (para: 33). When all of these perspectives impact on collaborative planning and teaching, the result can be exhilarating. Community musicians often bring to the music classroom an authenticity to the music-making experience within the genre in which they are experts. The following example demonstrates this.

---

### Case study: Jazz conventions within WCIVT

A jazz musician and instrumental tutor and class teacher are working collaboratively with a Year 5 Wider Opportunities class. The children have been learning trumpet and clarinets for almost a year and the class teacher is learning the trumpet alongside his class. The class teacher co-leads the aural/vocal activities planned and supports musical learning by developing these with the children throughout the week. They adopt an aural approach, modelling each process and demonstrating using the voice and instrument throughout the session. They begin with body percussion and vocal tasks to establish a feel for the pulse and the 8-beat timeframe within which the children will make music, and use copy-back tasks leading to call and response phrases. When the children are ready, they begin to use their instruments. The jazz musician performs rhythmic calls on one note which the children and the class teacher copy back. He increases the complexity with each musical phrase and the children copy accurately with a secure feel for the syncopation.

He then models the lead melody with distinctive feel and stylistic expression/interpretation which goes far beyond just the notes – this is imitated and 'caught' by the children in their responses as they get into that particular jazz groove. The authenticity of the musical experience and the immediacy of the teaching style leads to highly successful musical outcomes.

Towards the end of this one-hour session the children are performing confidently and stylistically as they create and present an extended piece based on these three main events: copy back, improvisation and the lead melody (which is extended and harmonised).

## How might we create and develop successful collaborations?

The starting place in planning a collaborative project or programme is to establish a 'shared vision'. Those involved will spend time getting to know the strengths, expertise and skills and levels of confidence of the collective team. This will involve discussion about the purpose and hoped-for outcomes for the project/programme and how best to achieve these, i.e. a pedagogical framework. What do we want the children to learn? What musical understanding will they develop? What are the musical experiences they will be involved in? Based on knowledge of the local context of the school, the children and their specific prior musical learning and experiences, interests and learning needs, the goals and outcomes which underpin this shared vision should be agreed and will provide the framework for future planning and teaching. See the following example.

### Case study: Collaborative planning in action

A school in East London has a multi-cultural intake with a marginal majority of white working-class children and is planning a Wider Opportunities programme. The initial idea comes from the music co-ordinator who is keen to establish increased musical opportunities for the pupils at this school. The teaching team consists of the class teacher and two instrumental teachers from the local music service. They meet prior to the start of the programme and begin by finding out about the team's expertise and levels of confidence in both teaching whole classes and teaching music, the children's musical experiences and learning to date and any specific musical or educational needs, talents or interests they may have. They discover that the class teacher is keen to lead vocal activities but isn't comfortable working with instruments in music lessons. One of the instrumental tutors is classically trained whilst the other has a rock/pop background. The class enjoy singing, though the concentration span of some of the six pupils on the SEN register sometimes leads to low-level disruption. There are five pupils from ethnic minority backgrounds who have musical experience within their cultures, for example the tabla, gospel singing and dhol drumming, and three pupils who are beginner violinists, one of whom has passed her Grade 1 examination.

Armed with this knowledge, the teachers begin to shape the scheme of work so that the learning objectives and outcomes, and activities planned to support these, meet the needs of those pupils with SEN and those who have instrumental expertise, take into account the cultural backgrounds of the pupils and differentiate in a range of ways so that all pupils can engage, make progress and enjoy the music-making opportunities.

Finally the team discusses how they will share the teaching within the lessons, agreeing that the class teacher will lead the singing activities whilst the instrumental teachers will take turns to lead specific activities with the instruments, but agree to review this at the end of each lesson. The scheme of work is placed on the music service website and the team agree to contribute to the development of each half-term unit over the coming weeks, focusing initially on the autumn term.

---

*Activity 14.3 Instigating a collaborative project*

Write a proposal to be submitted to your headteacher, head of music service or community music organiser outlining a planned collaborative project to take place with a particular year group. Identify the partners you would wish to work with, the experiences and expertise they will bring to the project and the project's musical focus and outcomes. Analyse how your choice of partners and musical focus addresses the local context of the school and particularly the children's prior musical experiences and learning. Think about how you will make time for effective joint planning.

---

The best collaborative programmes are organic and fluid, responding to both the children's engagement and progress and the team's collective imaginative and creative development. In the planning and teaching phases opportunities for continued input and sharing of ideas should be provided and created. One way to achieve this might be to use ICT to share and develop these plans over time, for example via a blog or a wiki. This approach to collaborative planning allows all those identified to take part in this process, ensuring it remains a living, developing, individualised and relevant programme.

Such an approach might be supported by frequent and regular meetings to review the children's progress, i.e. to assess and evaluate where the children are and focus on ways to move them forward and the repertoire to best support this. Within these meetings strategies for assessing pupil progress may be discussed. An increasingly common feature within whole class instrumental and vocal programmes is the development of the class teacher's role in assessing the children's musical progress.

## Conclusion

Working with other professionals can be a most inspiring and enriching experience and offers excellent opportunities for one's own professional development. Successful collaborations broaden musical and pedagogical horizons, skills and understanding, helping to break down barriers and develop an integrated approach to teaching and learning.

Practitioners may be inspired by the new genres and authentic music-making experiences, workshops and performances offered by the visiting 'specialist' or expert and feel challenged to learn new musical devices, approaches and skills, especially when the impact of musical learning on their pupils is strong. Class teachers can inspire others as they demonstrate their knowledge and understanding of whole class pedagogy, the children and their individual needs and ways to motivate and support them to learn.

When learning from each other is at the heart of a collaborative programme the potential for both teachers' professional development and children's musical learning is huge.

## Note

1 The Musical Futures Project is funded by the Paul Hamlyn Foundation: see www.musicalfutures. org.uk. It explores different approaches to music provision at KS3.

## References

Department for Education and Skills (DfES) (2006) *Music Manifesto Report No.2: Making Every Child's Music Matter*. London: The Stationery Office.

Ofsted (2009) *Making More of Music: An Evaluation of Music in Schools 2005/08*. London: Ofsted. Downloadable free from www.ofsted.gov.uk (accessed March 2010).

# Part 6

# Assessing, evaluating and reflecting

# Chapter 15

# Assessing, evaluating and reflecting

*Chris Philpott*

---

This chapter will focus on the way in which assessment can be used to ensure that all children involved in WCIVT receive their entitlement to a music education which meets their individual needs, supports their progression as musical learners and addresses their musical interests and aspirations. The chapter is based on the key principle that assessment is about teachers coming to know the musical understandings of their pupils (see Rowntree 1977) and using that knowledge as the basis for supporting their further musical development. It also involves pupils knowing themselves, and each other, as musicians. Assessment should be integrated into all teaching and learning since, as Swanwick suggests, 'to teach is to assess' (1988: 149). Additionally, assessment can be used to evaluate the effectiveness of our teaching and provide a basis for development and improvement.

In one sense music has been the most assessed of disciplines both in school and beyond, for example the 'pop' charts, graded examinations, competitions. Furthermore, we are all used to making judgements and critical comments about music of all types; we constantly assess music as part of our lives. However, this cultural experience has caused a rather skewed view of what counts as assessment in music education, i.e. that it is about making value judgements on musical products such as the quality of a particular performance or the latest album by our favourite band. This chapter will aim to establish a wider concept of what counts as assessment in music, how it might support children's access to, and inclusion in, the music curriculum and how it can be used to the advantage of whole class instrumental and vocal teaching.

When coming to know our pupils there are two broad ways of categorising assessment, *assessment for learning* and *assessment of learning*.

## Assessment for learning

Assessment for learning, sometimes referred to as formative assessment, is:

> any assessment for which the first priority is to serve the purpose of promoting students' learning … it is usually informal, embedded in all aspects of teaching and learning … (and this) becomes *formative assessment* when the evidence is use to adapt the teaching work to meet learning needs.
>
> (Black *et al.* 2003: 2)

Assessment activities which fall into this category are in one sense the most natural. Assessment for learning is about an ongoing dialogue about music between pupils and teachers and will include: *questioning*; *feedback*; *target setting*; *discussing criteria*; *self assessment*; *peer assessment*. Such assessment is pupil focused and aims to develop pupils' musical learning and understanding. This form of assessment is embedded in the process of teaching.

## Assessment of learning

Assessment of learning, sometimes referred to as summative assessment, involves 'tests that are infrequent, isolated from normal teaching and learning, carried out on special occasions with formal rituals' (Black *et al.* 2003: 2). Assessment here might include: *a written report on a pupil's progress; written and practical tests; an examination; giving marks and/or grades to work.* Such assessment is typically teacher focused and aims to ascertain the learning and understanding of pupils at a particular point (snapshot) in time e.g. the end of a unit of work carried out with a group.

Each of these broad categories are different ways in which we can know our pupils and for them to know themselves as musicians and learners. In this chapter we are going to focus primarily on 'assessment for learning' and particularly ways in which assessment can be integrated into WCIVT and not just 'bolted on'.

By the end of this chapter you will have considered how within all WCIVT sessions:

- you will get to know your pupils through questioning, feedback, self and peer assessment and the formative use of summative assessment;
- you will learn how to use assessment to develop and improve teaching.

## Approaches to assessment for learning

If to 'teach is to assess' then the assessment can be seen as the ongoing dialogue between pupil and teacher using the classic tools of assessment for learning noted above:

- questioning;
- feedback;
- self-assessment;
- peer assessment.

(Black *et al.* 2003)

Central to the dialogue (though not exclusively) is talk: talk between teachers, between pupils and between teachers and pupils. 'Teachers' here refers to the wider workforce in music education.

It is common for us all to talk about music; we know what we hear, we can describe it, can justify whether or not we like it and make suggestions for improvements. This is the talk of the workplace, the playground, the disco, the staffroom. Take the following example of a Year 6 pupil's description of 'O Fortuna' from Carl Orff's 'Carmina Burana':

This is dramatic! In the beginning there is a big drum then really loud but slow singing. It sounds all threatening and angry like a storm. Then suddenly the singing is faster and like a whisper but it still sounds really frightening like a horror film or a nightmare. But this does not last for long and the loud music comes back. It's in a foreign language and sounds like what monks would sing – I do not usually listen to music like this.

The language here describes the raw sound of the music, the expressive impact, the structure and even begins to locate it in their own musical tastes, without the use of any 'technical' language. Anyone can talk about music whether using technical or descriptive language or both, and this kind of talk can get to the very heart of pupils' individual needs and their musical interests and aspirations. The rationale of WCIVT validates the use of intuitive language in a conversation about music. Pupils learn in large groups with their peers and, in the most effective cases, also with their class teacher, and their conversations will be a natural part of their learning. Conversation is the life blood of assessment for learning.

How can the 'classic' tools of assessment noted above be integrated into WCIVT, where to teach is to assess?

## Questioning

Questioning is a vital strategy for coming to know our pupils. Brown and Edmonson suggest the following reasons for asking questions:

- to encourage thought and understanding of ideas and procedures;
- check understanding, knowledge and skills;
- gain attention and aid management;
- review, revise, recall and reinforce;
- teach the whole class through pupil answers;
- give everyone a chance to answer;
- use able pupils to encourage others;
- draw in shyer pupils;
- probe after critical answers;
- allow expression of feelings, views and empathy.

(Brown and Edmonson 1984 in Kyriacou 1991)

In relation to assessment for learning, the knowledge gained about pupils through questioning enables the teacher to adapt their responses in order to maximise the learning of each individual pupil. The assessment evidence derived from questioning can feed into planning for learning and teaching.

Most questions can be categorised as open/closed and high order/low order, as in Table 15.1.

Table 15.1 Question types

| Type of question | Example |
| --- | --- |
| Open question | In what other ways could we play this passage? |
| Closed question | What fingering do we use for D? |
| High order question | How does the music create a sad mood? |
| Low order question | What instrument plays the opening fanfare? |

Closed and lower order questions are almost always capable of leading to open and high order questions. Therefore, a question concerning the identification of musical style can then lead on to pupils being asked to justify their answer through reference to the music's stylistic features. It is likely to be the open and higher order questions that really cause your pupils to think about their learning, and thus effective questioning can be used as a tool to tailor your teaching as you come to 'know' your pupils. Of course, when using questioning to support access and inclusion, questions are not addressed to pupils in an arbitrary manner but are formed specifically for and directed to individual pupils in order to gauge their understanding and to allow them to demonstrate learning.

---

### Activity 15.1 Questioning and assessment

Observe a WCIVT led by an experienced colleague. Using the bullet points from Brown and Edmonson at the beginning of this section identify the different ways in which questioning is used. Consider also the teacher's use of closed and open questioning and how they ensure that all children have the opportunity to answer.

Before the next WCIVT session that you lead, decide how you might use questioning in a way that you have not done to a great extent, for example to allow pupils to express feelings, views and emotions. Plan exactly where in the session you are going to allow time for your questioning and plan a list of five questions that you might use with your WCIVT group. (You may not use these exact questions in reality but, by planning your questioning, you will elicit the sort of responses that you would like.)

---

### Feedback

An important part of assessment for learning is feedback. Vygotsky (1986) has justified the importance of feedback through a concept he called the *zone of proximal development* (ZPD). The ZPD is the gap between that which a pupil can understand on their own and their potential understanding in collaboration with teachers or capable peers, and of course is different for each learner. The support offered to 'close the gap' between these points is known as 'scaffolding', and feedback is an important scaffolding device to 'close the gap'. Good practice in feedback is individualised, identifies the current level of understanding, identifies areas for development and suggests ways in which these can be achieved.

An example of feedback in the context of WCIVT is outlined in Figure 15.1.

*Example 1*

1 Ben, you can now play C to G (on a trumpet) very securely. Well done!

2 I would now like to see if you can play these notes smoothly (legato) and spikily (staccato).

3 Listen to how I do this and then practise with Kas and Phil; try to use a sharp, spitting tongue (spiky) and a soft tongue (smooth).


*Example 2*

1 Aleya, that is a lively improvisation you have produced over the riff.

2 Do you think you might try to 'swing' the music a little more in keeping with the 'blues' style?

3 We can try this together or listen to Jono's group and join in with them or listen to this CD.


*Example 3*

1 Ali, you are singing this song with style and gusto!

2 We can now try to nail those long notes by thinking about where to breathe.

3 Read the words and decide the most natural places to breathe and then try this out with your group.

*Figure 15.1* Scaffolding in music to 'close the gap'

An important part of feedback and scaffolding in music is modelling. Indeed, part of the task to 'close the gap' could be for the pupils to listen to musical models played by the teacher or indeed to play or 'jam' with them. In some musical communities this is very common where the feedback is not spoken but happens all the time and as part of the teacher and pupil playing together.

> *Activity 15.2 'Closing the gap'*
>
> Using Figure 15.1, develop some of your own scenarios for 'closing the gap' which arise out of the work that you do. Remember that the 'scaffolding', i.e. the support to achieve the learning, can come from a variety of sources, including teacher models, pupil models, recorded models, questions (see above), suggestions and comments. When developing your scenarios, briefly describe the nature of the 'gap' that needs to be closed and the particular individual needs that it addresses.

When giving feedback or asking questions, teachers make active interventions in relation to pupils' work and this needs to be carefully judged. Teachers need to become skilled at sensing when pupils need, and are open to, intervention. If poorly judged, interventions can breed resentment, and a teacher always needs to operate on a spectrum from 'leave well alone' to more active involvement in the learning.

The effectiveness of feedback to pupils can also be enhanced if the criteria for success (the teacher's expectations) are shared with the pupils. Such criteria can include:

- criteria devised by the teacher for what counts as success;
- criteria devised by the pupils for what counts as success;
- criteria devised in collaboration between pupil and teacher;
- criteria derived in collaboration between teachers.

While it could be that teachers involved in WCIVT will be asked to use the National Curriculum levels, the most useful and effective criteria are those which arise out of the work being carried out by teachers and pupils themselves and in relation to what they believe to be a successful outcome for a lesson or unit of work. In this sense it is good to have local, learning specific criteria which have meaning for individual classrooms. Such local criteria could have the following features:

- they are clear and easily understood by all involved in making judgements (teacher and pupils)
- they are explicitly related to the aims and objectives of the learning themselves
- they focus on the musical outcomes although others can be included e.g. effort, social cooperation, etc.

> *Activity 15.3 Sharing assessment criteria*
>
> Using the work you have carried out in WCIVT, try to write some criteria for success that could be shared with your pupils and used as part of feedback and 'closing the gap' activities.

It is clear that if both teacher and pupil understand the criteria for success then feedback not only makes sense but can act as a reference point for target setting and closing the gap for individual pupils. Having said these things, teachers also need to be alert to unexpected musical outcomes which confound their expectations, and do not 'fit' with the criteria.

### Self-assessment

Sharing criteria is also vital to self-assessment and a key aspect of the use of assessment in meeting the principle of access and inclusion. If pupils understand and are aware of criteria then they can assess themselves, and this process has the following advantages:

- it actively engages pupils in their own learning;
- it facilitates ownership and autonomy in learning;
- it promotes the development of thinking skills;
- it promotes an understanding of *what* pupils have learned;
- it promotes an understanding of *how* pupils have learned.

Self-assessment needs to be carefully modelled for it to be successful. However, if we can encourage pupils to ask themselves the right questions and share with them the criteria for success, then the process has the potential to deliver significant gains in motivation and learning.

Self-assessment can also be instigated during feedback by using the questioning techniques noted earlier, as scaffolding. For example, as part of an improvising task pupils can be asked to reflect on their own learning by asking them the following:

1   What effects were you trying to achieve? What influenced your improvisation? How did the piece come about?
2   What did you learn by improvising in this piece as part of the whole group performance? What improvisation skills do you think you have developed?
3   How does the improvisation compare to others in the class? How does it compare to the original brief, expectations and/or criteria for success?
4   How has your approach to improvising developed as a result of this work? When do you make your best improvisations? What will help you to become a better improviser?
5   What might you do next?

---

*Activity 15.4 Self-assessment*

Choose a musical activity that you have carried out with a group in WCIVT. Design an evaluation postcard for your pupils to use which asks them to question and make comments on their learning. Remember to make reference to your own expectations (that were shared with them) and to use open and closed questions. The aim is for pupils to reflect on their understanding of what and how they have learned, and how their learning might progress further.

---

Self-assessment is intimately related to the peer assessment process.

### Peer assessment

Peer assessment has many of the benefits of self-assessment. In the case of improvisation where peers are assessing each other's work, they each gain a window onto someone else's solution to a musical 'problem', and thus gain a new perspective on their own work. Peer assessment, like self-assessment, needs a good deal of modelling and practice to make it work. Teachers in WCIVT should remember that the most effective assessment is focused on learning and that peers should be asked to comment on positive points and to make polite suggestions for development about each other's work. In this sense peers can act as teachers, offering each other feedback. While peer feedback *can* be based on criteria for success there is no necessity for peers to give an overall mark or grade. Black *et al.* (2003) conclude that grades and marks offered by *anyone* are of relatively limited value to learning.

### Integrating arts media into the assessment process

The principles of assessment for learning promote the notion that pupils are given opportunities to show and develop their understanding through a variety of media. To this end musical understandings can be witnessed when, for example, pupils make music, move to music and create a sculpture in response to music. As important as words are in the process of assessment if we only come to know our pupils through dialogue we might easily miss their intuitive and musical understandings. Some understandings can only be demonstrated when making music and in this sense music is the language that we 'speak' when composing and performing. There should always be opportunities for pupils to respond to music through music, for example, after they have listened to a piece of music. What might their response be to 'O Fortuna' in composition, improvisation or performance?

Having said this, musical is a highly abstract art and your pupils can benefit from translating their understandings into other artistic media. Musical understandings can be shown through dance (how might pupils move to 'O Fortuna'?); through art (what might they draw in response to 'O Fortuna'?); through drama (how can this music be acted out?).

### Summative assessment: collecting evidence and reporting

There are times when you will want to collect a summative 'snapshot' of your pupils, for example at the end of a series of sessions. Indeed, it is good practice to collect evidence for the musical achievement of your pupils in a wide range of forms. Here are some practical suggestions:

- audio, video and digital evidence of performances and compositions;
- self and peer assessments made by pupils;
- pupils' written assessments, e.g. evaluation postcards;
- 'jottings' made by you on significant features of the pupils' work, e.g. based on verbal responses gleaned during the dialogue of assessment for learning;
- a 'mark' book of attendance, comments, grades, etc.

Collecting and recording assessment evidence should be seen as part of the routine of teaching and be based on efficient strategies which do not undermine the process of learning. This evidence can then become the basis for a teacher's accountability and reporting to parents, line managers and external bodies. The important thing to consider is how to use the evidence as part of the process of feedback to your pupils in order to make formative use of the summative evidence.

## Assessment, evaluation and reflection

As we come to know our pupils, so we come to know the quality of the music education we have provided for them. As we integrate teaching and assessment, so we are given feedback on the effectiveness of our own teaching and how we need to adapt it in relation to the learning needs of individual pupils. Evaluation involves us in using assessment evidence to appraise the extent to which pupils have achieved our aims and objectives. Reflection engages the teacher in making decisions about how to respond to the results of evaluation. For example, upon playing along with our pupils, we might discover that some are finding it tough to hold a steady pulse. As a result of this we might reflect on a range of strategies to try in the next session. Do we use body percussion to help them 'feel' the pulse? Do we ask them to move to some music? Do we model pulse through playing along in close proximity to the pupils who are having problems? At the same time, pupils in the same group are able to weave some rhythmic improvisations around the pulse. Do we ask these pupils to 'buddy' another pupil as a performance partner? Do we build in their new-found musicianship into the whole class performance?

---

*Activity 15.5 Evaluating the effectiveness of your teaching*

Using the questions below as a guide, evaluate the effectiveness of your own teaching of a WCIVT lesson. Your response to all questions should be in the context of reflecting upon the effectiveness in terms of pupils' musical learning and the quality of their musical experience in the lesson. Note that the last question is a hugely important one.

---

When evaluating your own teaching you might ask the following questions:

- Did the pupils learn what you planned they should learn. Did other learning take place and if so how valuable was that learning?
- What is the evidence that pupils have learnt? Is this evidence musical evidence?
- What difficulties did any of the pupils experience. How did you recognise those difficulties and what did you do to address them?
- If pupils didn't achieve what you wanted them to, what was problematic. Was it the structure and timing of lessons? The level of challenge of the tasks and/or their appropriateness for the children being taught? The use of questioning?
- What do I need to do and what issues do I need to consider for future teaching in general and my teaching of this class in particular.

Through evaluation and reflection teachers show themselves to be accountable for the quality of their work to both themselves and their pupils. They also show accountability through collecting, recording and reporting evidence for the musical progress of their pupils. Evaluation and reflection is a natural consequence of the maxim 'to teach is to assess'.

## Conclusion

In summary, this chapter has argued that assessment is about WCIVT practitioners coming to know the musical understandings of their pupils and thus to be able to provide for their needs. It is also about pupils knowing themselves and each other as musicians and musical learners. When coming to know our pupils, assessment is integrated into the process of learning and teaching. Furthermore, the outcomes of the assessment process can be used to evaluate the effectiveness of teaching and provide a basis for its development and improvement.

What are the implications of this chapter for musical learning in WCIVT? It would seem that effective assessment for learning can take place when:

- music lessons predominantly involve pupils engaging with music in audience, as performers and as composers;
- there are opportunities for dialogue (verbal, musical and through other media) to take place as pupils compose, improvise and perform together;
- it is accepted that pupils bring their own understandings to any dialogue;
- WCIVT practitioners perform with their pupils;
- WCIVT practitioners compose with their pupils;
- WCIVT practitioners improvise with their pupils;
- WCIVT practitioners listen to music with their pupils.

The strategies of assessment for learning noted above allow pupils to behave musically and are flexible and open enough to capture the nuances of the discipline. If we believe that musical understanding is at the heart of musical learning then assessment for learning has a huge role to play when teachers facilitate and recognise this in WCIVT sessions. The aim is to allow pupils to develop as individual musicians and for teachers to come to know them as musicians. Each pupil has different needs, aspirations and interests. Assessment for learning supports both personal and collective engagement with music.

## References

Black, P., Harrison, C., Lee, C., Marshall, B. and William, D. (2003) *Assessment for Learning*. Milton Keynes: Open University Press.

Kyriacou, C. (1991) *Essential Teaching Skills*. Cheltenham: Nelson Thornes.

Rowntree, D. (1977) *Assessing Students: How Shall We Know Them?* London: Harper & Row.

Swanwick, K. (1988) *Music, Mind and Education*. London: Routledge.

Vygotsky, L. S. (1986) *Thought and Language* (rev. edn), trans. A. Kozulin, Cambridge, MA.: MIT Press.

# Index

Page numbers follwed by 'f' refer to figures and followed by 't' refer to tables.

# eBooks

eBooks – at www.eBookstore.tandf.co.uk

## A library at your fingertips!

eBooks are electronic versions of printed books. You can store them on your PC/laptop or browse them online.

They have advantages for anyone needing rapid access to a wide variety of published, copyright information.

eBooks can help your research by enabling you to bookmark chapters, annotate text and use instant searches to find specific words or phrases. Several eBook files would fit on even a small laptop or PDA.

**NEW:** Save money by eSubscribing: cheap, online access to any eBook for as long as you need it.

## Annual subscription packages

We now offer special low-cost bulk subscriptions to packages of eBooks in certain subject areas. These are available to libraries or to individuals.

For more information please contact webmaster.ebooks@tandf.co.uk

We're continually developing the eBook concept, so keep up to date by visiting the website.

## www.eBookstore.tandf.co.uk